Business Studies and Economics
FOR THE PACIFIC

OF ESSENTIAL TERMS

BRIAN DEUTROM

Oxford University Press is a department of the University of Oxford.

It furthers the University's objective of excellence in research, scholarship, and education by publishing worldwide. Oxford is a registered trademark of Oxford University Press in the UK and in certain other countries.

Published in Australia by
Oxford University Press
253 Normanby Road, South Melbourne, Victoria 3205, Australia

First published 2015
Reprinted 2021

ISBN 978 0 19 559688 5

Illustrated by diacriTech, Chennai, India
Typeset by diacriTech, Chennai, India
Printed by Golden Cup Printing Co. Ltd

Preface

Business Studies and Economics for the Pacific: A–Z of Essential Terms has its origins in a commerce dictionary published more than 15 years ago to provide high school students in the Pacific with a list of the terms to support their studies in commerce. In developing this book I have reviewed and revised those terms, deleted those that are no longer relevant and added others, such as those relating to e-commerce, that have now become an integral part of modern business.

The major change, however, is the inclusion of concepts and terms that students will need to understand to successfully complete their economics course of studies. These concepts have been approached in a simple and practical manner and are supported with graphs, diagrams and tables presenting information of both regional and international relevance. This book also includes a series of headwords dealing with what can be called global climate change (GCC) issues. The socio-economic implications of GCC are among the most important economic debates of the present and the near future.

Business Studies and Economics for the Pacific: A–Z of Essential Terms contains more than 1900 entries, more than 70 figures and calculations, guides to the pronunciation of difficult words, and bold terms highlighting and linking words related to a concept or topic. This book provides high school students of business studies and economics with a comprehensive list of terms to support their studies. Tertiary students and those undertaking further studies in accounting, banking and insurance may also find this book a useful resource.

BRIAN DEUTROM
Torquay, UK
March 2014

Dedicated to Sophie, Grace, Yasmin and Zipporah

abnormal item

in a set of accounts, an item of revenue and expense, and other gains and losses, resulting from ordinary operations but considered abnormal because of its size and its effect on the results for the period. See **extraordinary item**.

abnormal profit

permanently high profits earned by a monopoly because there is no competition. See **monopoly**.

abnormal returns

the difference between the actual return and the expected return under normal conditions.

absenteeism

the practice of regularly staying away from work or school without good reason.

absolute advantage

the ability of an individual, firm or country to produce more of something with the same amount of effort and resources than any other individual, firm or country.

ABV

acronym for Australian Business Volunteers – an Australian volunteer organisation aimed at helping business and government organisations in developing countries. Formerly known as Australian Executive Service Overseas Programme (AESOP).

acceptance of offer

a document stating that an offer that has been made has been accepted. An acceptance of offer is necessary to make a contract legal.

accident insurance

insurance policy that will provide compensation for accidental bodily injury or death.

account

1 a record or statement of financial transactions relating

to an individual or asset such as is kept in a bank, retail store or brokerage.

2 An arrangement between a buyer and seller in which payment is made at some time in the future.

account payee only

when 'account payee only' is written between two parallel lines on a cheque, the cheque can be banked only into the account of the person to whom the cheque has been made payable. See **bearer cheque**, **crossed cheque**, **Fig. 1** (below).

account rendered

a bill that has been sent but not yet paid. An amount of money that is overdue for payment.

accountability

the obligation of an individual or organisation to account for its activities, accept responsibility for them, and disclose the results in an honest manner. It also includes the responsibility for money or other entrusted property.

accountant

a person who keeps or inspects financial records.

accounting

the process or work of keeping financial records.

accounting concepts

the principles and rules of accounting that have to be

Figure 1 Account payee only

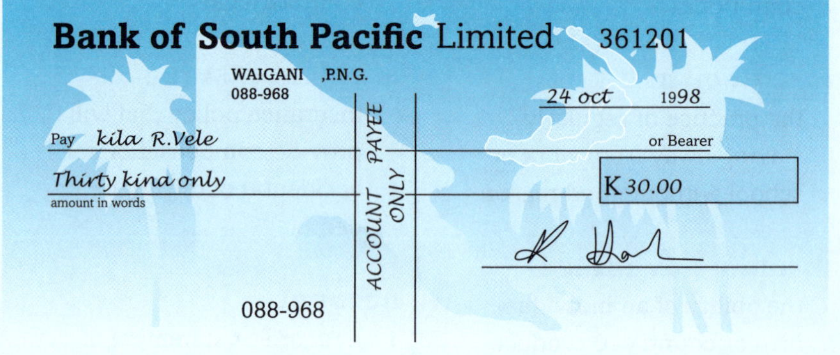

Figure 2 Accounting equation

Capital or shareholder equity = Total assets – Total liabilities

followed in the preparation of accounts and financial statements.

accounting entity

an economic unit such as a business or section of a business, for which separate accounts are maintained.

accounting equation

the foundation of double entry bookkeeping. An equation for calculating a company's capital or shareholder equity. Capital or shareholder equity is equal to total assets minus total liabilities. See **capital**, **liabilities**, **Fig. 2** (above).

accounting framework

the accounting principles used in the preparation of the profit and loss account and balance sheet. See **accounting concepts**, **financial statement**.

accounting manual

a manual that contains accounting rules and other information for a business or organisation. It explains what should be entered into each account in the ledger.

accounting period

the period for which books are balanced and the financial statements are prepared. Usually the accounting period is 12 months but could be 1 month or 6 months. See **financial statement**.

accounting period concept

the idea that financial (profit and loss) statements need to be prepared at regular periods of time, which are called the accounting period. See **accounting period**.

accounting principles

See **accounting concepts**.

accounting rate of return (ARR)

also known as the simple rate of return. The ratio of profit to capital (investment) expressed as a percentage. Investors or business owners use projected ARRs to compare the possible profits for proposed projects, products or investments. See **Fig. 3** (below).

accounting records

all records, such as invoices, statements, payment vouchers and receipts, that are used in preparing the financial statements. See **financial statement**.

accounting reports

periodic statements showing the financial position of a business over a given period of time or at a given time. The main accounting reports are the annual financial statement, profit and loss report, balance sheet and cash flow statement for the whole business.

accounting standards

the accounting principles of a country, which are used as a reference to determine how various matters in the preparation of the profit and loss account and balance sheet should be dealt with. See **international accounting standards**.

accounting system

the particular accounting system that each firm uses to prepare its annual financial statements, profit and loss account and balance sheet.

accounts

a record of all the financial transactions of a firm, usually for a year. It includes the profit and loss account and balance sheet.

accounts for directors

the profit and loss account and balance sheet prepared for the use of directors in a company and not necessarily for shareholders.

accounts payable

money owed by a business to its creditors. See **creditor**.

accounts receivable

the outstanding amounts owed to a business as a result of

Figure 3 Accounting rate of return

$$\text{ARR} = \frac{\text{Net profit}}{\text{Capital or investment}} \times 100\%$$

sales or services provided to customers. See **debtor**.

accrual [uh-**kroo**-uhl]
accumulating or adding together. See **accrual accounting**.

accrual accounting [uh-**kroo**-uhl]
a method of accounting that includes amounts for liabilities not yet paid out and cash owing to a company not yet received at the time of the preparation of financial statements. See **accounts payable**, **accounts receivable**, **accrual**, **accrued expenses**, **accrued revenue**.

accrued expense [a-**krood**]
expense incurred during the accounting period but not yet paid at the end of the period. See **accounts payable**, **accrual accounting**.

accrued revenue [a-**krood rev**-uhn-yoo]
also called accrued income. Income earned from sales and services provided during the accounting period but not yet received at the end of the period. See **accounts receivable**, **accrual accounting**.

accumulated depreciation [uh-**kyoo**-myuh-leyt-ud dih-pree-shee-**ay**-shn]
total depreciation of a fixed asset up to a point of time. The depreciation for the current period added to the depreciation for all other previous periods. See **depreciation**.

accumulated fund [uh-**kyoo**-myuh-leyt-ud]
the equivalent of a capital account for a non-profit organisation.

acid test [**as**-id]
the test of whether a business can pay those of its debts that are immediately payable. See **quick assets ratio**.

acid test ratio
See **quick assets ratio**.

acquisition
one company taking over the controlling interests of another company. See **merger**.

acronym
an abbreviation formed from the first letters of other words and sometimes pronounced as a word. For example, *a.s.a.p.* is an acronym for *as soon as possible.*

act of God
events outside human control, such as cyclones, earthquakes, sudden floods or other natural disasters. Events for which no one can be held responsible.

Act of Parliament
a law passed by Parliament. See **bill**.

actuary [**ak**-choo-er-ee]
a person employed by an insurance company, who calculates insurance risks and premiums by analysing the statistics of risk factors such as climate change (in relation to floods and storms), death rates, accidents, fires and thefts.

ADB
See **Asian Development Bank**.

added value
the difference between the selling price of a good or service and the cost of inputs such as materials and components. Wages, taxes, etc. are deducted from the added value to give the profit. See **value added**.

addendum
additional information at the end of a report or book.

adding value
increasing the value of resources by changing them during the production process.

address
the name and place of business to which a letter or parcel is sent. In countries such as Papua New Guinea, where there is no mail delivery service, letters are addressed to post office box numbers. See **post office box**.

addressee
the name of the person or business to whom a letter or parcel is addressed.

adequate disclosure
clear, full and accurate information regarding a company's financial position, such as financial statements,

so that the reader can make a proper assessment before investing in the company or providing credit. See **financial statement**, **footnotes**.

administrator

a person who carries out the administration of a business or organisation.

ad valorem tariff

Latin for 'according to value'. A tariff levied as a percentage of the price of an import.

ad valorem tax

Latin for 'according to value'. A tax on a good or service levied as a percentage of its value. VAT is an example of an ad valorem tax. See **VAT**.

advance

payment received for goods or services before the goods or services are delivered or performed. When the business receives an advance payment, it records it as a liability.

adverse selection

the tendency of those who are at highest risk to take out insurance.

advertise [**ad**-ver-tyz]

describe or draw attention to a product, or service in a public medium (such as newspapers, radio, television, the Internet or posters and billboards) in order to create consumer interest and promote sales.

advertisement [ad-ver-**tyz**-muhnt]

a notice or advice in a newspaper, radio, television, the Internet, poster or billboard that describes and draws attention to a product or services.

advertising [**ad**-ver-ty-zing]

1 the profession of producing advertisements for commercial products or services.

2 the act of using paid announcements in newspapers and magazines, over radio or television, on billboards, or through the Internet, to make the public aware of a product or service. The aim of advertising is generally to get more customers and therefore increase demand. However, negative advertising such as information on the dangers of smoking tobacco is aimed at

Figure 3a Result of positive advertising

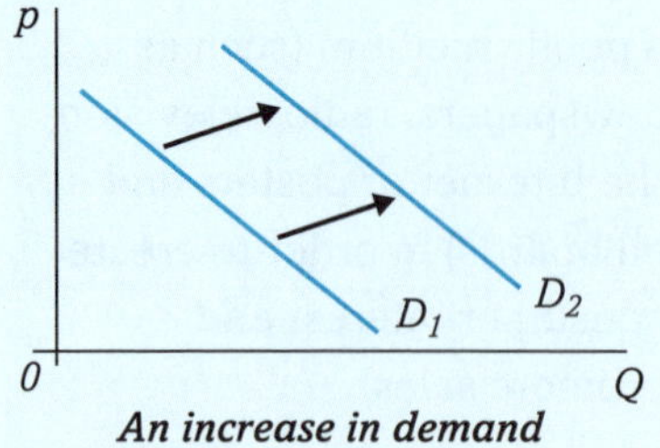

Figure 3b Result of negative advertising

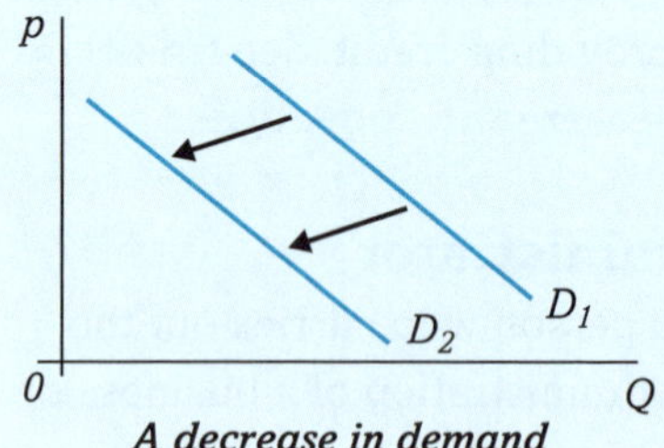

reducing consumer numbers and therefore reducing demand. See **Figures 3a** and **3b** (above).

advertising media

the different means – such as newspapers, billboards, television, radio and the Internet – by which advertisements can be communicated to consumers.

advertising elasticity of demand (AED)

[ih-la-**stis**-i-tee]

a measure of the effect on demand caused by a change in spending on advertising. AED is calculated as the ratio of the percentage change in demand for a good or service to the percentage change in advertising spending. AED is usually positive, with increased advertising resulting in increased demand. Negative advertising such as information on the dangers of smoking will (hopefully) have a negative AED. See **advertising**, **elasticity**, **Fig. 4** (below).

aerogram [**air**-uh-gram]

a self-stamped, lightweight sheet of stationery that folds

Figure 4 Advertising elasticity of demand

$$\text{AED} = \frac{\%\,\text{change in quantity demanded}}{\%\,\text{change in spending on advertising}}$$

into its own envelope for mailing at a low postage rate.

affordability
[uh-fawr-duh-**bihl**-i-tee]

1 expenditure by a business is affordable if it generates income to cover operational, maintenance and financing costs. See **appropriate capital**, **cost blowouts**, **overspending**.
2 deciding whether an expenditure by a family or individual is affordable is not as easy to make. A simple way to look at affordability in this case is to ask if the expenditure will make the purchase of essential household needs difficult.

after-sales service
meeting customers' needs and providing them with support such as maintaining or fixing equipment after a product or service has been purchased.

ageing of debtors [**ey**-jing] [**det**-erz]
the process of listing accounts receivable (debtors) showing the length of time each invoice has been outstanding.

ageing population
[pop-yuh-**ley**-shn]
a characteristic of the age distribution of population in a developed country. Falling birth rates and death rates result in an increase in the average age of the population and a greater proportion of older people. See **age-sex pyramid**, **population pyramid** and France in **Fig. 5** (p. 10).

agenda [uh-**jen**-duh]
a list of matters to be discussed at a formal meeting.

agent
a person who acts on behalf of another person in a business transaction, such as the sales and distribution of a good or range of goods.

age–sex pyramid
[**pir**-uh-mid]
a type of graph showing the distribution of a country's population by age group and sex. See **ageing population**, **population pyramid**, **Fig. 5** (p. 10).

Figure 5 Age–sex pyramids of a developed country (France) and a developing country (India)

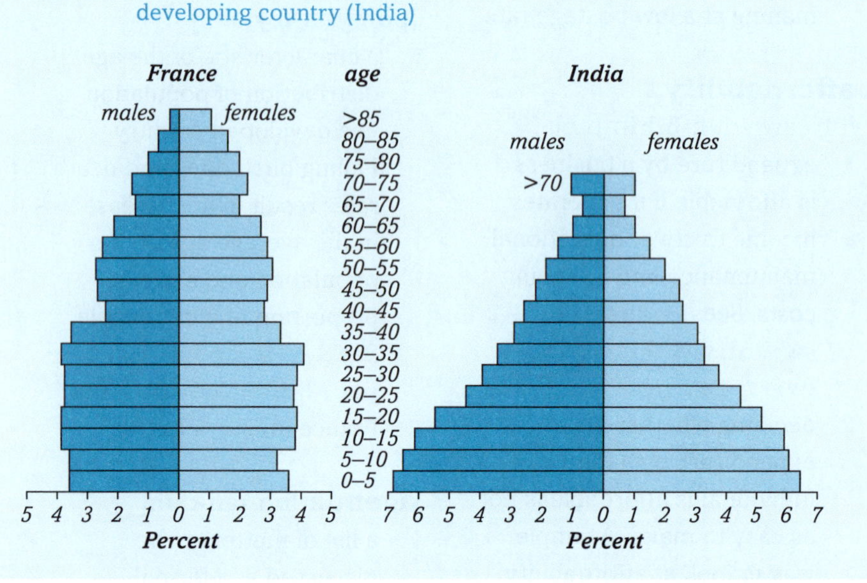

agglomeration [uh-glom-uh-**rey**-shn]

benefits that businesses obtain by locating near each other ('agglomerating'). Even when competing companies agglomerate, such as in the 'Chinatown' district of many Pacific cities, there are advantages because the cluster attracts more suppliers and customers. Cities develop and grow to exploit the economies of agglomeration. See **external economies of scale**, **network effects**.

aggregate [**ag**-ri-geyt]

the sum or total.

aggregate demand [**ag**-ri-geyt dih-**mahnd**]

the total quantity of all goods and services demanded by the economy at a given time and price level. It is made up of the sum of consumption (C), investment (I), government spending (G) and the difference between exports (X) and imports (M). See **aggregate demand curve**, **Fig. 6** (p. 11).

Figure 6 Aggregate demand

$$AD = C + I + G + (X - M)$$

aggregate demand curve

a graphical representation of the total quantity of all goods (and services) demanded by the economy at different price levels. Falling prices usually result in increased demand. See **aggregate demand**.

aggregate supply

the total supply of all goods and services produced within an economy at a given time and price level. It is represented by the aggregate supply curve. See **aggregate supply curve**.

aggregate supply curve

a graphical representation of the relationship between price levels and total output of all goods and services for the whole economy. Rising prices usually result in firms expanding their production. See **aggregate supply**.

aggregate demand for labour curve

a graphical representation of the total demand for labour in the economy at different levels of real wage rates.

aggregate supply of labour curve

a graphical representation of the total number of people willing and able to work at different average real wage rates.

agriculture sector

the part of the economy comprising farming, animal husbandry, fishing, forestry and hunting. See **primary sector**.

AIDS

the disease caused by the human immunodeficiency virus (HIV). After becoming infected with HIV a person may not develop the AIDS disease for up to 15 years. The word AIDS comes from the first letters of 'acquired immune deficiency syndrome'. Also called HIV/AIDS, it is a condition in which the immune system fails, allowing life-threatening infections and cancers to take over the body. People do not die of AIDS but from other diseases such as cancer or TB, because their bodies lose resistance to these diseases. PNG is in the early stages of a serious epidemic of HIV/AIDS. The long-term influence of this epidemic is difficult to predict. However, the experience of rural East Africa suggests that it will have significant socio-economic effects, particularly on food and cash crop production, and on the wellbeing of children in rural communities. This is because the people most likely to become infected are young adults, who produce, feed and care for children. Drugs that control the virus and improve the body's immune system to resist infection are available in the Pacific region but are very expensive. See **HIV**, **HIV positive**, **antiretroviral drug**.

airmail

transporting mail by aircraft.

air transport

a system of moving passengers and goods by aircraft.

air waybill

also called a consignment note. A receipt issued by an air freight company on receipt of goods, agreeing to deliver the goods to a destination. The freight company will release the goods to the consignee (person to whom the goods are addressed). See **bill of lading**, **consignee**.

alienated land

land that has been acquired from customary landowners by the government, either for its own use or for private development. The colonial governments alienated land in all former colonies in the Pacific region. See **customary land**.

allocation of resources

resources are in limited supply and human wants are unlimited. Decisions therefore have to be made as to how the limited resources are used. In a free-enterprise or market economy, price, supply and demand direct these decisions. The resources are used to produce goods that are most desired by consumers. In a planned economy and in the public sectors of a mixed economy, decisions regarding resource use and distribution are political. See **basic economic problem**, **capitalism**, **centrally planned economy**, **economics**, **free enterprise**, **market economy**, **mixed economy**.

allotment of shares
the creation of shares in a company and their transfer to shareholders. See **share**, **shareholder**.

alphabetical filing
[al-fuh-**bet**-i-kuhl]
a filing system in which documents are arranged in alphabetical order form A to Z. See **file**.

alternate [**awl**-ter-neyt]
a person who attends a meeting in the absence of a member of a committee or board of directors in a company. This person must be appointed as another person's alternate.

alternative energy
[awl-**tur**-nuh-tiv]
energy produced by means other than the burning of fossil fuels such as coal, oil and gas. Examples include solar, hydroelectric, wind, tidal, geothermal, nuclear energy and biofuels such as ethanol and biodiesel. See **carbon trading**, **climate change**, **greenhouse gas**, **renewable energy**.

alternatives
[awl-**tur**-nuh-tivz]
options from which to make choices. See **choice**, **criteria**, **decision making**.

amendment
a formal change to a document or record such as a motion, bill, or Constitution. See **bill**, **Constitution**, **motion**.

amalgamation
[uh-mal-guh-**mey**-shn]
a merger of two or more companies. See **merger**.

amortisation
[uh-mawr-ty-**zey**-shn]
1 the practice of reducing the value of assets to reflect their reduced worth over time. Amortisation and depreciation have the same meaning. However, the term amortisation is usually used

for the write-off of intangible assets. See **amortisation of goodwill**, **depreciation**.

2 the reducing of a debt by paying both interest and principal.

amortisation of goodwill

the annual writing-off for tax purposes in a company's balance sheet of the initial cost of goodwill See **goodwill**, **write-off**.

annual general meeting

the yearly meeting required to be held by companies and clubs, where shareholders or members receive reports detailing the financial and other activities undertaken during the year. New directors or executives may also be elected during the meeting. See **agenda**, **annual report**.

annual report

the yearly evaluation report, including financial statements (profit and loss account and balance sheet) and footnotes, a letter from the president and other helpful information to evaluate the financial position and performance of the company. The annual report is presented to shareholders, potential investors, creditors, regulatory bodies such as the Registrar of Companies and others interested parties.

annual return

1 a yearly statement giving information on the company's composition such as the board of drectors and shareholders, activities and financial position that must be sent to the Registrar of Companies or other appropriate authority.

2 the percentage yearly return on an investment.

annuity [uh-**noo**-i-tee]

an asset, grant or allowance that pays an individual an amount annually, for a fixed period of time or for the person's lifetime.

answering machine

a tape recorder or digital device that provides a recorded response to a telephone call when there is no one to answer the telephone. The caller has the option to leave a recorded message, which can later be played back by the person receiving the call.

anti-competitive practices
[an-tee-kuhm-**pet**-i-tiv]
business or government practices that prevent or reduce competition in a market. See **collusion**, **collusive oligopoly**, **collusive tendering**, **dividing territories**, **dumping**, **exclusive dealing**, **limit pricing**, **monopoly**, **price fixing**, **refusal to deal**, **resale price maintenance**, **tying**.

antiretroviral drug
[**an**-ti-re-truh-vy-ruhl]
a group of medications that are used as treatment for HIV infection. The drugs control the multiplication of the virus in the body but are very expensive. See **AIDS**, **HIV**.

apology
notification given to a meeting by a person who cannot attend.

app (apps)
See **mobile application**.

appendix
additional information at the end of a report or a book.

applicant
a person who has put in a formal application for something such as a job, entry to school or a loan.

application
1 the formal request, usually a letter, asking to be considered for something such as a job, entry to school or a loan.
2 a computer program that has been designed for a particular use, such as a database, word processor or web browser program. See **computer software**.

application form
1 a form on which an application for a job can be made.
2 a form used to apply for a service, such as obtaining a passport or visa, or applying for credit from a company.

application software

See **computer software**.

appraisal [uh-**pray**-zuhl]

a method of measuring the performance of an employee. These are usually carried out once a year.

appreciation [uh-pree-shee-**ay**-shn]

the increase in the value of an asset which is due to economic or other conditions and not because of improvements or additions made to it. It is the opposite of depreciation. See **depreciation**.

appro

abbreviation for *on approval*. Goods on appro can be returned if they are not what the buyer wants.

appropriation account [uh-proh-pree-**ay**-shn]

the final section of a profit and loss account that shows how the profit of the business are to be used, including distribution among partners or shareholders.

appropriate capital [uh-**proh**-pree-yet]

capital that improves productivity, is suitable for the needs of the producer and is affordable. A new machine that improves working conditions and matches production requirement is an example of appropriate capital. A new machine that produces 5,000 units a day when 10,000 is required in an example of inappropriate capital. See **affordability**.

appropriate technology [tek-**nol**-uh-jee]

technology that is suitable to the local social and economic conditions, is environmentally sound, and promotes self-sufficiency. Labour-based technologies in the building and maintenance of rural roads in Pacific countries has proved to be cost-effective and provide much needed rural employment.

aptitude test

a test used in the recruitment process to test specific skills of an applicant.

arbitrage [**ahr**-bi-trahzh]
the purchase of an asset such as currencies, shares, securities, or commodities in one market (country) where it has a lower price and selling it in another market (country) where it has a higher price and thereby making a profit. Unequal prices often result from differences in foreign exchange rates.

arbitrage opportunity [**ahr**-bi-trahzh]
an opportunity to buy an asset at a low price and sell it almost immediately in a different market for a higher price. See **arbitrage**.

arbitration [ahr-bi-**trey**-shn]
the process by which the parties to a dispute submit their differences to the judgment of an impartial person or group appointed by mutual consent or by law.

arc elasticity [ahrk ih-la-**stis**-i-tee]
the ratio of the percentage change of one variable to the percentage change in another variable. The percentage changes in the two variables are calculated relative to the value at the midpoint between the original and final values. See **elasticity**, **Fig. 39** (p. 103).

arc elasticity of demand
the ratio of the percentage change in quantity demanded of a good or service to the percentage change in its price, as calculated by the arc method. See **arc elasticity**, **elasticity of demand**, **Fig. 39** (p. 103).

arc elasticity of supply
the ratio of the percentage change in quantity supplied of a good or service to the percentage change in its price, as calculated by the arc method. See arc **elasticity**, **elasticity of supply**, **Fig. 39** (p. 103).

articles of association
the internal rules of a company. In some countries, these have been replaced by the constitution of a company. See **constitution**.

a.s.a.p.
acronym for 'as soon as possible'.

Asian Development Bank
a regional development bank whose aim is to facilitate economic development of countries in Asia and the Pacific. See **World Bank**.

Asia–Pacific Economic Cooperation (APEC)
an association of 21 Pacific Rim states that seeks to promote free trade and economic cooperation throughout the Asia–Pacific region. APEC works to remove trade tariffs and other obstacles to trade in the area and raise living standards and education levels through sustainable economic growth. Papua New Guinea is a member of APEC. See **World Trade Organization (WTO)**.

asset [**ass**-et]
resources of economic value owned by a company or individual. In accounting there are two types of assets, namely current assets and fixed assets:

1 current assets include cash, accounts receivable and inventory. See **current assets**.
2 fixed assets include such things as equipment, buildings and real estate. See **fixed assets**.

asset backing per share
the net assets of a company, divided by the number of ordinary (or equity) shares issued.
See **asset**, **share**, **Fig. 7** (below).

asset revaluation reserve [ree-val-yoo-**ay**-shn]
an amount entered into a balance sheet, equal to the

Figure 7 Asset backing per share

$$\text{Net assets} = \text{Total assets} - \text{Liabilities}$$

$$\text{Asset backing per share} = \frac{\text{Net assets}}{\text{Number of shares}}$$

increase in value of fixed assets such as buildings and land. See **fixed assets**.

asset stripping
taking over a company in financial difficulties and selling each of its assets separately at a profit.

ATM
acronym for *automatic teller machine*. See **acronym**, **automatic teller machine**.

auction [**awk**-shn]
a public sale in which goods or property are sold to the highest bidder. Residential and commercial properties are often sold at an auction.

auctioneer [awk-shuh-**neer**]
a person who conducts an auction.

audit [**aw**-dit]
an official examination of the annual accounts of a company or organisation. The result of an audit is an audit report stating whether the financial records are in order and whether the profit and loss account and balance sheet show a true and fair view. See **audit report**, **true and fair view**.

auditor [**aw**-di-ter]
a person or company who audits accounts. See **audit**, **true and fair view**.

audit report
a signed document which gives the result of the audit. The report may include the findings, conclusions or opinions of the auditor and make recommendations.

audit trail
a list of transactions in the order they occurred. A step-by-step record by which financial or other business data can be traced to its source.

authorised capital
also called authorised share capital, registered capital or nominal capital in some countries. The maximum amount of share capital that the company can, under its constitution, allocate to shareholders. Part of the authorised capital can remain unissued as shares. The part of the authorised

capital that has been issued to shareholders is referred to as the issued capital of the company. See **issued capital**.

automatic teller machine (ATM)

an electronic machine that provides banking services when activated by insertion of a plastic card. Also called a cash machine or cash point. The customer may be drawing money from an account or receiving an advance, or loan. See **ATM**, **credit card**, **debit card**.

automatic payment

an arrangement with a bank to have regular withdrawals made from an account to pay recurring bills such as loan repayments and rent.

automation

[aw-tuh-**may**-shn]

the replacement of labour by machines.

average collection period

the average amount of time it takes for a business to receive payments of monies owed by clients and customers.

average cost

total cost for all units bought (or produced) divided by the number of units. See **weighted average cost**.

average fixed cost (AFC)

the total fixed costs of production (FC) divided by the quantity of output produced (Q). Fixed costs are those costs that must be incurred in fixed quantity, regardless of the level of output produced.

$$AFC = \frac{FC}{Q}$$

As the total number of units of the good produced increases, the average fixed cost decreases, because the same amount of fixed costs is being spread over a larger number of units of output. See **average total cost**, **average variable cost**, **fixed costs**.

average product

a measure of productivity with a certain number of workers. A factory that produces 100 units a day with 10 workers has an average product of 10 units per worker.

Figure 8 Average rate of return

$$\text{Average rate of return} = \frac{\text{Average annual return}}{\text{Initial cost of investment}} \times 100\%$$

average rate of return (ARR)

a method of comparing investments by comparing expected average annual profit over the life of the project with the initial cost of investment. See **rate of return**, **Fig. 8** (above).

average revenue

total revenue from sales divided by number of units sold. If all units are sold at the same price the average revenue is equal to the sale price. Also called average revenue per unit (for a good being sold) or average revenue per user (of a service being provided).

average total cost (ATC)

also called unit cost. Equal to total cost of production divided by quantity (Q) of outputs produced. It is also equal to the sum of average variable cost (AVC) and the average fixed cost (AFC). See **average fixed cost**, **average variable cost**, **unit cost**, **Fig. 9** (below), **Fig. 24** (p. 71).

Figure 9 Average total cost

$$\text{ATC} = \frac{\text{AVC} + \text{AFC}}{\text{Q}}$$

average variable cost

equal to the total variable costs of production divided by the quantity (Q) of outputs produced. Variable costs are those costs that change in proportion to the quantity of goods or services produced. See **average fixed cost**, **average total cost**, **variable costs**, **Fig. 25** (p. 71).

backdate

1 to give something an earlier date than the current date, such as dating a document with an earlier date than the actual date on which the document was prepared.

2 to say that something began or became effective at a date earlier than the current date. For example, an increase in an employee's salary could be backdated to the beginning of the year.

back order

customers' orders that cannot be filled, usually because goods are not in stock. Back orders are shipped to the customer as soon as goods become available.

back up

1 to make a duplicate copy of original computer files on a separate data storage media. Backing up ensures that the data contained in a file is still available if the original file is damaged or lost.

2 the storage media (usually a hard disk) on which copies of the files and data are stored.

backward integration

[in-ti-**gray**-shn]

See **vertical integration**.

bad debt

a debt that cannot be recovered and is therefore written off in the ledger. See **written off**.

bad debt recovered

An account that was written off as a bad debt but was later paid by the customer. See **bad debt**.

balance

1 the difference between total debits and total credits in a ledger account.

2 amount remaining in a bank account.

3 the remainder of a loan yet to be repaid.

balanced budget

a budget in which total expenditure equals total

revenue. If expenditures are less than revenue there is a budget surplus. If expenditures are greater than revenue then there is a budget deficit. See **budget deficit**, **budget surplus**.

balance of payments (BOP)

the aggregate of all financial transactions by both the private and public sectors that take place between a country and the rest of the world over a period of time. Calculated every quarter and each calendar year, the BOP is a measure of how much money is coming into the country (credit) and going out (debit). The BOP is rarely balanced and tells whether the country has a deficit or surplus. The two main components of the BOP are the current account and the capital account. See **current account**, **capital account**.

balance of trade (BOT)

the difference between the value of a country's exports and imports of goods and services. If a country has a balance of trade deficit, the country imports more goods and services than it exports. If a country has a balance of trade surplus, the country exports more goods and services than it imports. See **balance of payments**, **balance of trade deficit**, **balance of trade surplus**, **trade gap**, **visible exports**, **visible imports**, **visible trade**.

balance of trade deficit

when the value of the goods and services exported is less than the value of the goods and services imported.

balance of trade surplus

[**ser**-pluss]

when the value of the goods and services exported is greater than the value of the goods and services imported.

balance sheet

a statement of the assets, liabilities and the owners' equity (capital) of a business at a point of time.
See **asset**, **capital, equity, liability, Fig. 10** (p. 24), **Fig. 11** (p. 24).

ballot

a method of voting secretly and in writing.

Figure 10 Balance sheet equations

In a balance sheet:

Assets = Owners' equity (capital) + Liabilities

or

Owners' equity (capital) = Assets – Liabilities

ballot box

a sealed box into which voters put their voting papers.

ballot paper

a slip of paper on which a voter writes his or her secret vote.

ballpark figure

an approximate estimation, made without complete information or detailed calculation.

bank

a financial company that is licensed to receive deposits from customers. There are two types of banks, commercial and investment banks. In most countries banks are regulated by government or by a central bank. See **central bank**, **commercial bank**, **investment bank**, **online bank**.

bank bill

a short-term money market investment instrument, generally between 30 and 180 days. A bank bill will usually be purchased by an

Figure 11 Sample balance sheet of a small business

Assets		*Liabilities and owners' equity*	
Cash	$6600	**Liabilities**	
Accounts receivable	$6200	Loan account	$5000
Tools and equipment	$25000	Creditors	$25000
		Total liabilities	$30000
		Owners' equity	
		Capital stock	$7000
		Retained earnings	$800
		Total owners' equity	$7800
Total	$37800	*Total*	$37800

investor at a discount, paying less than its expected value when it matures. See **bill of exchange**.

bank charges
fees and other charges customers are required to pay banks for their services.

bank cheque
See **bank draft**.

bank draft
also called a bank cheque or banker's draft. A cheque drawn by a bank against its own funds and bought by a person to pay a supplier who will not accept a normal cheque. The bank guarantees to pay the money. Such cheques cannot be dishonoured. A bank cheque is used in large transactions and where a creditor wants to be sure that the debtor can pay the debt.

bank loan
money lent by a bank to a customer to be repaid with interest before a fixed date. Repayments are often made as regular fixed payments. See **bank overdraft**.

bank manager
the person in change of a local branch of a bank.

bank overdraft
a type of bank loan that allows a person or company to continue withdrawing money, even if their account has no funds in it. Interest is charged on the overdrawn amount, on a daily basis.

bank reconciliation statement
[rek-uhn-sil-ee-**ay**-shn]
a statement that shows the reasons for the difference between the bank statement balance, according to the bank's records, and the customer's bank balance in the ledger. The difference could be due to the fact that, at any particular date, cheques may be outstanding, deposits may be in transit to the bank or errors may have occurred. See **bank statement**, **Fig. 12** (p. 26).

Figure 12 Bank reconciliation statement

Balance on bank statement		498.67
Less unpresented cheques		
Cheque no. 114	10.50	
Cheque no. 118	11.11	
		21.61
Balance on bank account ledger		477.06

bank statement

a record, usually sent once per month, to the holder of a bank account. It lists all transactions in the account from the time of the previous statement to the date of the current statement. It is the ledger account of the customer, in the bank's records.

banker

a person who manages or owns a bank.

bankrupt [**bangk**-ruhpt]

when a person or a company has liabilities greater than their assets. The person or their creditors can then file to have them declared bankrupt. A person who is a bankrupt cannot do certain things such as obtain credit or be a director of a company.

bankruptcy [**bangk**-ruhpt-see]

a legal process involving a person or business that is unable to repay outstanding debts. See **bankrupt**.

barcode

a group of printed numbers and thick and thin lines or shapes representing data about an object, which can be read by a scanner. Commonly used by supermarkets for automatic checkout, barcodes are now used for many different tasks and can even be read by smartphones. See **checkout**, **smartphone**, **Fig. 13** (p. 27).

Figure 13 Barcode

bargain

1 something bought or offered for sale at a price much lower than would normally be expected.

2 to negotiate.

3 an agreement between two individuals or groups as to what each will do for the other.

bargaining

a type of negotiation in which the buyer and seller of a good or service disagree and make offers and counter-offers on the price to be paid and the exact nature of the service. They eventually come to an agreement. See **collective bargaining**, **counter-offer**, **haggle**, **negotiate**.

barriers to market entry

anything that prevents or makes it difficult for new companies to enter a market. This limits the amount of competition faced by existing companys in the industry. See **anti-competitive practices**.

barriers to trade

restrictions on exports or imports imposed by a government to protect domestic industries against imports or prevent the export of essential items or native species. The barriers can include tariffs, import and export licenses, import quotas, subsidies for local exporters and restrictions on direct foreign investment. See **free trade**, **General Agreement on Tariffs and Trade (GATT)**, **protectionism**, **World Trade Organization (WTO)**.

barrister

lawyer who advises clients and can represent them in the higher courts. See **lawyer**, **solicitor**.

barter

a system of exchange in which goods or services are exchanged for other goods or services without the use of money.

barter economy

an economy in which people exchange goods or services directly with one another without any payment of money. Workers are paid with goods or services.

base period

the point in time chosen as the point of reference for comparison in the construction of an index such as the consumer price index (CPI). The base period is used as the beginning or reference period and its value is usually given as 100. All future periods are compared to the base period. See **consumer price index (CPI)**, **retail price index**, **price index**, **Fig. 24** (p. 67).

base-weighted index

the average price of an individual good or service or a group of goods and services, as compared to the average price of the same good, service or group of goods and services at some previous set time called the base period. See **base period**, **basket**, **consumer price index (CPI)**, **price index**, **retail price index**.

basic economic problem

also called the economic problem. The fundamental economic theory stating that in any economy resources are scarce and insufficient to satisfy all human wants and needs. The problem is more simply explained by the question 'how do we satisfy unlimited wants and needs with limited resources?' See **allocation of resources**, **economics**.

basis points

given as 0.01% in yield. For example, in increase in yield on an investment from 6.00% to 6.05% is said to increase by five basis points.

basket

a group of fixed quantities of known goods or currencies, used for defining a price index or exchange rate. See

consumer price index (CPI), **fixed exchange rate**, **price index**, **retail price index**.

bearer cheque

a cheque drawn on a bank by a holder of a current account at that bank. The bank will pay the amount of money specified to any person who presents the cheque to the bank. See **account payee only**, **order cheque**.

bear

investor who thinks the market or the value of a specific share will decline. An investor who is a 'bear' will sell stock (take a short position), believing that they can be buy the stock back later at a lower price. A bear market is one in which the prices of stocks are falling. See **bulls**, **futures contract**, **long**, **options contract**, **selling short**, **short**.

beneficial externalities

See **positive externalities**.

beneficiary [ben-uh-**fish**-uh-ree]

a person who will receive something from another person. For example, the person who receives an inheritance upon the death of another person.

benefits in kind

benefits received by employees other than their usual cash salary. They include such things as a company car, subsidised housing, health insurance and free or subsidised meals. See **fringe benefits**, **net advantages of a job**, **perks**.

bequeath [bih-**kweeth**]

to leave money or property to someone in a will. See **beneficiary**, **will**.

bequest [bih-**kwest**]

1 the act of giving or leaving money or property in a will. See **bequeath**.

2 the money or property that is given in a will. See **legacy**.

biannual [by-**an**-yoo-uhl]

twice a year.

biennial [by-**en**-ee-uhl]

every two years.

bilateral foreign aid

[by-**lat**-er-uhl]

aid given by one country directly to another country.

bill

1. a printed or written statement of monies owed for the purchase of goods or services. See **invoice**.
2. a draft of a proposed law presented to Parliament for discussion. See **Act of Parliament**.
3. a term used in America to mean a bank note, such as in a '*ten dollar bill*'.
4. sometimes used as a term for bill of exchange or bill of lading. See **bill of exchange**, **bill of lading.**

bill of exchange

a document or certificate signed by one party agreeing to pay a stated amount of money to a second party on a certain date. Bills of exchange are often used for making payments in foreign trade. Bills of exchange can to transferred or sold to a third party. See **Fig. 14** (below).

Figure 14 Bill of exchange

No 801 30 December 2014

Thirty days after date, pay this bill of exchange to the order of Papua New Guinea Banking Corporation, Port Moresby, the sum of ten thousand kina payable at the current rate of exchange.

To N.Z Trading Co Ltd
Karangahape Road
Auckland, New Zealand

For and on behalf of
POM Trading Co Ltd
A. IEWAGO, Manager
A. Iewago

The importer's bank presents the bill to N.Z Trading Co Ltd for acceptance. The usual form of acceptance (written across the face of the bill) is as follows: Accepted Payable at Bank of New Zealand, Auckland.

bill of lading
a legal document between the shipper of goods and the carrier, which details the type, quantity and destination of the goods being shipped. Similar to an air waybill except that the consignee (person to whom the goods are addressed) needs to present original documents before receiving the goods. See **air waybill**, **consignee**.

bill of sale
written document that transfers goods, title or other interests from a seller to a buyer and specifies the terms and conditions of the transaction.

birth rate
the number of births per year for every 1000 people in the population.

bitcoin
a digital or virtual currency (also called crypto-currency) that is not backed by any country's central bank or government. There are no physical bitcoins, only electronic balances that are kept on a public ledger. Bitcoins can be traded for goods or services with vendors who accept bitcoins as payment or kept as a store of value or wealth. Like any other currency, the value of bitcoins changes in relation to other formal currencies. Anyone wishing to own bitcoins needs to open a computer-based 'Bitcoin wallet' and then either buy bitcoins online using traditional currencies or accept online payment in bitcoins for goods or services.

Many governments are suspicious of bitcoins because they can be owned and used anonymously to transfer illegal funds such as the earnings of drug dealers or used to hide income from taxation authorities. The Chinese government has banned institutions from accepting payment in bitcoins. Other governments such as those of the USA and India have warned against their use and are cracking down on 'black markets' that accept payments in bitcoins for the sale of illegal goods. Nonetheless, the use of bitcoins is gaining popularity. The first bitcoin ATM where individuals can buy or sell bitcoins for cash opened in Sydney, Australia in 2014. See **ATM**, **exchange rate**, **function of money**, **medium of exchange**, **money**, **store of value**.

black market

1 the illegal business of buying or selling goods such as illegal alcohol without paying taxes and duties, or against government restrictions such as price control or rationing.

2 place where these illegal operations are carried on.

board meeting

a meeting of the board of directors of a company or organisation, which is usually held once each month.

board of directors

a group of persons elected by a company's stockholders to run the business. The board usually consists of top management executives and representatives from outside the company.

bona fide [**boh**-nuh fyd] also [**boh**-nuh fy-dee]

Latin term meaning honest, sincere, lawful or legal.

bond

1 a debt investment in which an investor lends money to a corporation or government for a defined period of time at a fixed interest rate. Periodic interest is usually paid.

2 cash given to assure satisfactory performance. For example, a landowner of a property may require a tenant to deposit a bond assuring that there will be no damage caused to the property.

3 goods in a bonded warehouse are said to be under bond and will not be released until the customs duty is paid. See **bonded warehouse**.

bonded warehouse

a warehouse at a seaport or airport that is authorised by a country's customs department to store goods for which customs duty has not yet been paid. The goods are released when the customs duty is paid.

bonus
an extra payment made to employees in recognition of their good work.

book value
the amount shown for an asset in the ledger of a company. For example, the book value of a piece of machinery at a particular time is its initial cost less the accumulated depreciation. Book value is more correctly called the carrying value. See **carrying value**.

bookkeeper
a person who keeps the records of the financial transactions of a business.

bookkeeping
the process or occupation of keeping a record of the financial affairs of a business

boom
a period of time during which sales of a product or business activity increases very rapidly. In the stock market, booms are associated with bull markets. See **bull**, **bull market**.

borrow
to receive something that belongs to someone else on loan for a period of time before returning it. Money borrowed usually has to be repaid with interest.

bounced cheque
a cheque that has been written for an amount greater than the account balance and is not honoured by the bank because of the insufficient funds. See **dishonour**, **dishonoured cheque**, **refer to drawer**, **represent**.

box number
also called a PO box number. The number of a mailbox at a particular post office to which mail can be addressed.

branch
any location other than company's headquarters where business activities of the company are carried out.

brand
a name given by a business to one or more of its products, so that it can be identified by the customer. The brand

name is often registered as a trademark. For example, Coke or Nike. See **intangible asset**.

brand image

opinion or impression of a particular brand of product held by consumers/customers. A product with a strong brand image is more likely to have an inelastic demand curve. See **inelastic demand**, **intangible asset**.

brand loyalty

a situation in which some consumers continue to buy a brand of goods they are familiar with, have bought before or seen in advertising rather than the same goods produced by a competitor.

breach of contract

failure by either party to a contract to do something that is required under the contract.

break even

when a business sells just enough product to cover its costs. See **break-even point**.

break-even point

the point where total revenue and total cost are the same. See **Fig. 15** (below).

Figure 15 Break-even point

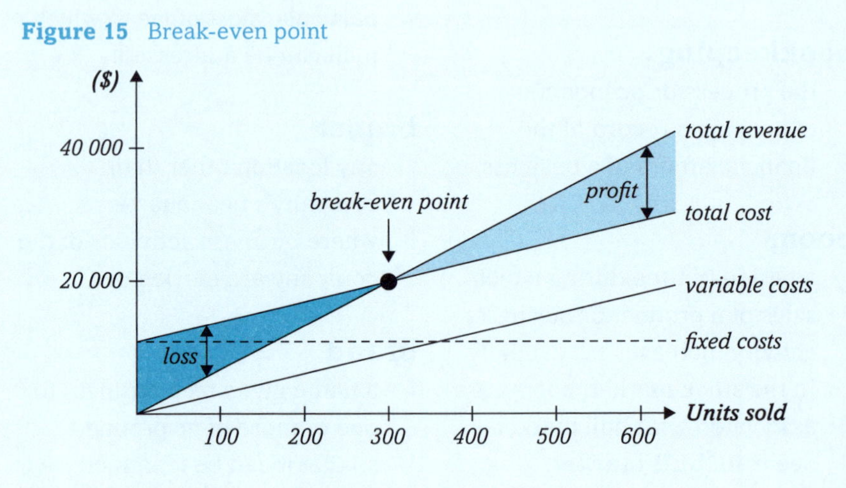

break-even point of production

the quantity of units of production which when sold will result a zero profit and no loss. See **Fig. 15** (p. 34).

broker [**broh**-ker]

1 an agent who buys and sells for others.

2 a member of a stock exchange who buys and sells shares and bonds on behalf of clients.

brokerage [**broh**-ker-ridje]

1 the business of a broker.

2 the fee or commission paid to a broker.

3 a company that buys and sells stocks and bonds for clients.

brought forward

acknowledging that a value from one accounting period, such as an accumulated balance, has been brought forward at the start of a new accounting period.

browser

a software application used to locate and display content on the World Wide Web, including webpages, images, video and other files. See **Internet**, **webpage**, **World Wide Web**.

bubble

a period of fast-rising prices of stocks or other commodities such as house prices, usually above their true value. Also called a 'boom'. In the stock market a bubble is usually associated with a bull market and is always followed by a dramatic drop in prices, caused by mass selling. See **bear**, **boom**, **bull**, **business cycle**, **bust**, **Fig. 16** (p. 37).

budget

1 in a business the budget is an economic plan prepared from estimates of the various types of income, expenses, assets to be purchased, loans to be made, and loans to be repaid. A budget is prepared at least annually and used for planning and control purposes.

2 in government, the budget is the annual financial plan showing detailed costings for government programs

and government's estimated tax and non-tax revenue. See **budget deficit, budget surplus**.

budget deficit

a situation where planned government spending is greater that government's estimated tax and non-tax revenue. In such a situation the government will need to borrow money to undertake its plans. See **balanced budget**, **budget surplus**.

budget surplus

a situation where a government's estimated tax and non-tax revenue is greater than planned government spending. See **balanced budget**, **budget deficit**.

building society

a financial organisation that pays interest on investments by its members and lends capital for the purchase or improvement of houses.

bulk buying

purchasing goods in large quantities, usually at a discount.

bull

investor who thinks the market or the value of a specific share will increase. An investor who is a *bull* will buy stock (take a long position) believing that they can sell the stock at a higher price. A bull market is one in which the prices of stocks are increasing. See **bear**, **futures contract**, **long**, **options contract**, **short**.

bull market

a market in which share prices are rising or expected to rise, thereby encouraging buying. See **boom**, **bull**.

business

1 an organisation such as a company that undertakes, commercial, industrial or professional activities.
2 a person's occupation, work or trade, as in 'what is your business?'
3 commercial activity, as in 'this company does business with Australia'.

business cycle

a pattern followed over a period of years by variables (such as GDP and

Figure 16 Business cycle

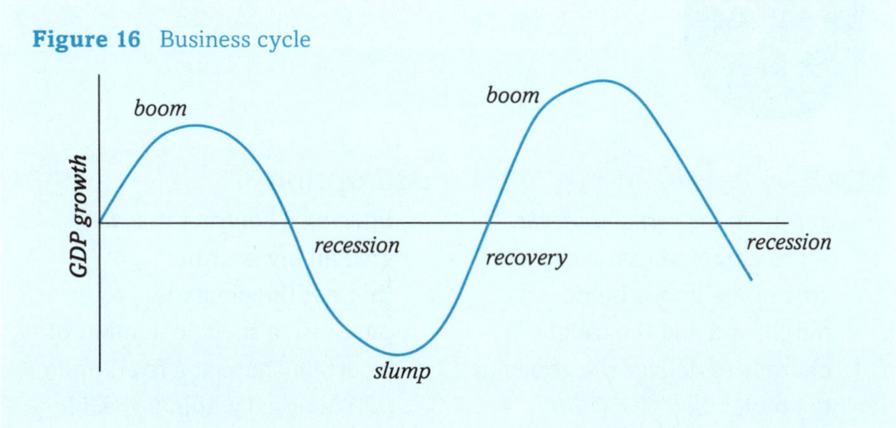

unemployment) that rise and fall irregularly over time, with periods of boom and recession. See **cyclic unemployment**, **Fig. 16** (above).

business reply post

a pre-addressed, reply-paid card or letter. The business sending it out has already paid the postage, so no postage stamp is required.

bust

a period of rapidly falling prices in stocks or other commodities such as house prices. A 'bust' always follows a period of rapidly rising prices (boom) and in the stock market is usually associated with a bear market. See **bear**, **boom**, **bubble**, **bull**, **business cycle**.

by-laws

the rules of a club, society or association.

by-product

a product that is produced in addition to the main product. Sawdust is a by-product of the production of timber. Coconut meat is a by-product of the production of coconut oil.

CAF

acronym for *cost and freight*. A price quoted that includes cost of the goods being purchased and the freight charges to deliver the goods to the buyer. See **CIF**, **FOB**.

calculator

a small electronic machine on which commercial and mathematical calculations can be made.

call

See **call option**.

call centre

a physical place where telephone calls from customers or telemarketing calls to customers are handled by operators working for, or on behalf of, an organisation. Many large corporations in developed countries outsource their customer communications to call centres in countries like India and the Philippines. See **outsource**, **telemarketing**.

call option

offering a contract that will give an investor the right (but not the obligation) to purchase a specific number of a certain share at a fixed price (strike price) within a specific time. Investors selling the contracts are required to pay a non-refundable premium for the right.

For example, if an investor believes that a share currently valued at $10 will rise in price to around $20, she can offer a call option contract to buy the shares at $15 each within three months. She offers a premium of $1 per share upfront to anyone buying her option. If the stock does rise to $20, the investor has the right to buy the shares for $15 each and make a profit of $5 per share on the contract, minus (of course) the premium $1. If the share does not reach $20, then the investor can decide not to exercise her right and simply lose her $1 premium.

See **derivative**, **options contract**, **put option**.

capital [kap-i-tl]

1 financial capital – money available for investment.
2 real capital – goods and infrastructure such as factories and ships that are used in the production of other goods or services. In economics, capital is classified as one of the four main factors of production. See **factors of production**.
3 in accounting, capital is total assets less total liabilities. See **accounting equation**.

capital account

measures investment flowing into and out of a country. Investments include purchase of land, buildings, mines, shares and bonds, deposits in banks and loans.

A surplus in the capital account means money is flowing into the country and represents borrowings from overseas and the purchase of national assets by overseas investors.

A deficit in the capital account shows money is flowing out of the country, and could mean that the nation is increasing its ownership of foreign assets.

The International Monetary Fund (IMF) and the World Bank split what the rest of the world calls the capital account into the financial account and capital account, with most of the transactions being recorded in the financial account. See **balance of payments**, **current account**.

capital asset

an asset purchased for use in production over a long period of time, rather than for quick resale. Capital assets include:

1 land, buildings, plant and equipment, mineral deposits, timber reserves.
2 patents, goodwill, trademarks, leaseholds.
3 investments in other companies.

capital commitment

the allocation of funds for a planned large capital expenditure such as the purchase of an asset of considerable worth.

Companies must disclose their capital commitments in notes (footnotes) accompanying a company report and balance sheet.

capital consumption
[kuhn-**sump**-shn]

an estimate of the loss in the value of capital equipment due to wearing out, breaking down or becoming obsolete because of new technologies. Capital consumption needs to be deducted from a country's GDP or from the profits of a company because it represents the amount of new investment needed to maintain the same level of production. See **depreciation**.

capital controls

laws that control how capital can be invested and resources allocated in an attempt to reduce capital flight and preserve foreign exchange. Examples include:

- foreign investors in Iceland were blocked from selling their assets following a banking crisis in that country in 2007.
- citizens in Cyprus were limited to withdrawing from, or writing cheques against, their bank accounts, for no more than €300 per day after that country's debt crisis in 2012.
- Ukrainian citizens were limited to USD$5800 in foreign exchange, and then only after a six-day waiting period, as a result of the political and economic crisis in that country in 2014.
- Argentinean citizens are required to pay an extra tax when vacationing abroad.

See **capital flight**, **foreign exchange controls**.

capital expenditure
[ik-**spen**-di-cher]

money spent by a company to acquire or upgrade physical assets such as property, industrial buildings or equipment. See **fixed asset**, **non-current asset**.

capital flight

the sudden large-scale movement of financial assets out of a country by residents and foreigners. Causes of capital flight include:

- fear of public disorder, persecution or physical danger to owners.
- unfavourable domestic economic circumstances such as large increases in taxation or fears of high inflation.

See **capital controls**.

capital formation

an increase during an accounting period of capital stock such as equipment, buildings and other intermediate goods. Capital formation results in an increased capacity for production.

capital gains

the profits that an individual or company makes when they sell a fixed asset for a price that is higher than its purchase price. See **capital gains tax**.

capital gains tax

a tax levied on profits made by individuals and companies from the sale of fixed assets. Circumstances such as adjustments for inflation, the age of the asset and the length of time between purchase and sale are all considered in calculating the tax liability. See **capital gains**.

capital good

a durable good (one that does not easily wear away) used in the production of goods and services that are bought by consumers. Buildings, equipment and machinery are examples of capital goods. See **capital asset**, **intermediate good**, **producer good**.

capital intensive

a business process or an industry that requires large amounts of money and other financial resources to produce a good or service. The air transport industry is an example of a capital intensive industry.

capitalisation

1 in accounting, the inclusion of costs incurred to acquire an asset in the price of an asset. For example, the cost of transporting a new machine would be added to its purchase price when calculating the value of the asset.

2 the market capitalisation of a company – calculated by multiplying the number of shares by the current trading value of each share.

3 a technique used by real estate agents to estimate the value of a property by using the annual rental income for a property.

capitalism

an economic system based on private ownership of capital and the use of that capital for the production of goods and services for profit. The production of goods and services is controlled by supply and demand in the open market – it is not centrally planned by government.

The majority of the population living under capitalism buy the things that they consume with money gained by selling the goods and or services they produce. See **centrally planned economy**, **communism**, **inequality**, **subsistence economy**, **welfare state**.

capital market

markets for buying and selling equity and debt instruments. Participants including individual investors, institutional investors such as pension funds and mutual funds, municipalities and governments, companies and organisations, and banks and financial institutions.

Capital markets are increasingly interconnected in the globalised economy. This means that problems in one country can spread around the globe. The collapse of the US mortgage-backed securities in 2007 spread quickly around the world causing the global financial crisis of 2007–2009. This was because banks and other institutions in Europe and Asia held trillions of dollars of these securities.

capital movements

the flow of capital across international boundaries, for investment in plant and machinery, or in response to interest rate changes or expectations of interest rate changes. See **capital flight**.

capital resources

goods such as buildings, equipment, and machinery that are used to produce other goods and services.

carbon offsetting

making those who emit the greenhouse gase carbon dioxide (CO_2) into the atmosphere pay for the external cost of their pollution by funding other activities that avoid or capture the equivalent equal amount of gas. For example, the owners of a fossil-fuel-burning power plant that emits CO_2 could be forced to build or fund wind-powered or solar-powered generators that avoid the emission of the same amount of CO_2. See **carbon pricing**, **carbon tax**, **emissions trading**, **externalities**, **photosynthesis**.

carbon pricing

putting a price on external costs resulting from the emission of CO_2. It is a way of making polluters, such as owners of factories and power plants, pay for the CO_2 they emit. The intention is that putting a price on CO_2 emissions will encourage companies to reduce their emissions in order to reduce costs. Carbon offsetting, carbon tax and emissions trading are all methods of carbon pricing. See **carbon offsetting**, **carbon tax**, **emissions trading**, **externalities**.

carbon tax

a tax paid by owners of factories and power plants on the amount of greenhouse gases they release into the atmosphere. The tax provides an incentive for them to use renewable-energy methods of production such as solar, hydroelectric or wind energy. The tax also provides governments with funding to undertake mitigation activities to protect against the effects of climate change and to support and subsidise the use and development of renewable energy technologies. See **emissions trading**, **fossil fuel**, **solar energy**, **wind power**.

career

an occupation or profession with opportunities for progress and advancement, which can be undertaken for a large part of a person's working life.

cargo

goods carried by aircraft, ship or motor vehicle.

carrying value

the value of an asset as shown in the balance sheet. Sometimes referred to as the book value. It is the original purchase cost of the asset, minus accumulated depreciation. See **book value**, **historical cost**.

cartel

agreement between a group of businesses or countries who are major producers of a certain good or service, to influence prices by limiting their production and/or fixing prices. See **anti-competitive practices**, **OPEC**.

cash

legal tender (money) in notes or coins that can be exchanged for goods, services or debt.

cash accounting

a method of accounting in which receipts and expenses are recorded in the period in which they are received or paid.

cash book

1. a book where records of cash, cheque receipts and cheque payments are kept.
2. in a computerised ledger, the bank account is sometimes referred to as the cash book.

cash crop

crops grown for sale rather than for the use of the grower.

cash cow

a business, or part of a business, that generates a steady, dependable flow of cash.

cash discount

a reduction in the price of an item if payment is made by a certain date.

cash earnings

the excess of cash revenues over cash expenses. This is different from other earnings as it doesn't include non-cash expenses like depreciation or amortisation.

cash float

a cash reserve that is added to the cash register at the start of each day to provide change to customers. See **cash register**.

cash flow

the total amount of money received and paid out. The difference between the money received and the money paid out is called the net cash flow.

cash flow analysis

an analysis that compares cash coming into and going out of a business during a specific period of time. The analysis begins with a starting balance and ends with an ending balance, after accounting for all cash receipts and expenses paid during the period. Such an analysis gives a good indication of the ability of a business to keep operating. See **cash flow forecast**.

cash flow budget

a budget of the cash flow. See **Fig. 17** (below).

Figure 17 Cash flow budget

	Kina
Balance at bank 1/1/15	10 000
Add estimated cash receipts from sales	110 000
	120 000
Less cash expenses (detailed)	(88 000)
Less purchases of fixed assets	(15 000)
Balance at bank 31/12/15	**17 000**

Note: The above budgeted cash flow budget would be prepared in detail and prepared on a month by month basis.

cash flow forecast

an estimate of the future cash inflows and outflows of a business, usually on a monthly basis.

cash flow statement

an accounting statement that shows the amount of cash generated (inflows) and used (outflows) by a company in a given period of time. Inflows arise from financing such as borrowing, sales and returns from investments. Outflows includes all expenses and investments. A cash flow statement is a good indication of a company's financial strength.

cash on delivery (COD)

a system of paying for goods when they are delivered. This means that the delivery and payment take place on the same date.

cash payments journal

a journal in which all cash payment transactions made by a business are recorded.

cash point

See **ATM**.

cash receipts journal

a journal in which all cash received by a business for goods and services are recorded.

cash register

also called a till. A mechanical or electronic device that calculates and records all cash sales transactions and has a drawer attached for storing cash.

cash sale

a sale that is paid for at the time of the sale. When a business refers to *cash sales* it is referring to the proportion of all sales paid for with cash.

cash transaction

a transaction that is settled with cash on the same day as the trade.

cashier

an employee who handles payments and receipts in a shop, bank or other business.

casual labour

workers on temporary employment, who usually

have limited benefits such as sick leave and have little or no security of employment.

caveat [**kav**-i-at]

1 a clarification, warning or caution.

2 a process in a court of law to temporarily stop proceedings, until some matter in relation to the action has been resolved.

caveat emptor [**kav**-i-at **emp**-tor]

Latin term meaning 'let the buyer beware'. It means that the buyer is responsible for checking the quality and suitability of goods before they make a purchase.

CD

acronym for compact disc. A circular plastic optical device designed for recording, storing, and playing back audio, video, and computer data. See **CD-ROM**, **disc**, **disk**.

CD-ROM

a compact disc (CD) on which the information stored cannot be changed or added to. ROM is the acronym of *read only memory*. See **CD**, **read only memory (ROM)**.

central bank

also known as the reserve bank or monetary authority of a country. It is the bank of the government that manages a country's currency, money supply and interest rates. The Bank of Papua New Guinea, the Reserve Bank of Vanuatu and the Central Bank of Solomon Islands are examples.

central government

a government of a nation-state that has the power to make laws for the whole country. See **local government**.

centralised

a management structure in which most decisions are made at the higher levels of management.

centrally planned economy

an economy in which the government, rather than the free market, determines the allocation of resources. Government decides what goods should be produced, how much should be produced and the price at which the goods will be offered for sale. The production of goods and services is often undertaken by state-owned enterprises. See **communism**.

central processing unit

See **CPU**.

CEO (Chief Executive Officer)

the highest-ranking executive in a company, who is responsible for the overall operations and performance of the company and reports to the board of directors.

certificate of deposit (CD)

certificate issued by banks for fixed-term interest-bearing deposits. They can be sold by the owner to another investor.

certificate of origin

document that states the place where items being imported were originally made. A certificate of origin is often a legal requirement if sensitive merchandise such as military equipment is being imported. See **end-user certificate**.

certified accountant

a qualified member of a legally recognised professional body of accountants. The levels of membership designate the qualifications and experience of the accountant.

For example, the Institute of Chartered Accountants in the United Kingdom, Canada, Australia, India, and several other British Commonwealth countries allow ordinary members to use the initials ACA (Associated Chartered Accountant) after their name. Those who have passed additional examinations are admitted as fellows and use the initials FCA (Fellow Chartered Accountant) after their name. The equivalent professional in the US is a certified public accountant (CPA).

Certified accountants are authorised to provide an audit opinion on the correctness of a company's financial statements.

certified financial statements

financial statements that have been audited and certified by a certified public accountant (CPA). See **certified public accountant**.

ceteris paribus [**key**-te-rees **pah**-ri-boos]

Latin phrase which literally means 'with other things the same'. Commonly understood as 'all other things being equal'. When carrying out an investigation to identify the relationship between variables, a scientists would change one variable at a time while keeping all the others variables constant (*ceteris paribus*). The scientist is then able to focus on the effects of that one factor in what is otherwise a complex situation.

Similarly, in economics, when one is studying the effects of one change (such as a change in price) it is important that nothing else (such as income, taste or the price of other goods) changes.

chain of command

the structure within an organisation that allows instructions to be passed down from senior management to the lower levels of management.

chain of production

the steps that need to be taken in order to transform raw materials into goods that can then be used by consumers. Value is added at each step of the production chain through the addition of inputs such as raw materials, labour, buildings, manufacturing, processing, distribution and marketing. See **inputs**, **outputs**, **transformations** and **Fig. 18** (p. 50).

change in demand

See **change in quantity demanded**, **determinants of demand**.

change in supply

See **change in quantity supplied**, **determinants of supply**.

Figure 18 Chain of production

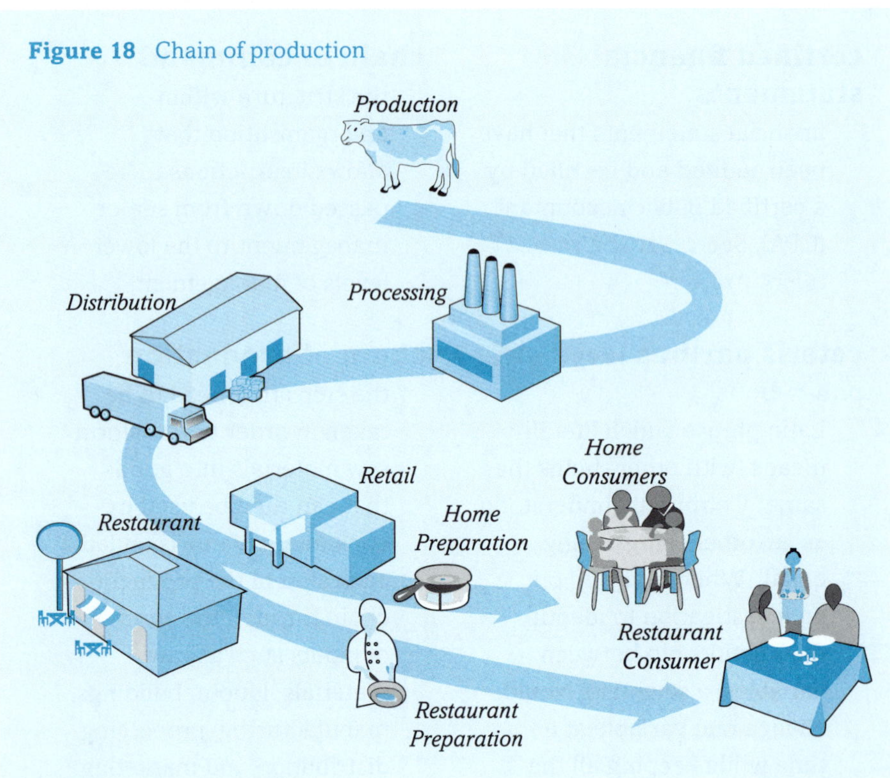

change in quantity demanded

an increase or decrease in the quantity of goods or services that are demanded at a given point of time, as represented by a change from one point on a demand curve to another point. This occurs when there is a change in price. See **demand curve**, **detriments of demand**, **Fig. 31a** (p. 85).

change in the quantity supplied

an increase or decrease in the quantity of goods or services that are supplied at a given point of time, as represented by a change from one point on a supply curve to another point. This occurs when there is a change in price. See **demand curve**, **detriments of supply**, **Fig. 31a** (p. 85).

changes in equilibrium
market forces (the pressures of demand and supply exerted by buyers and sellers) cause prices to change. If either supply or demand changes and the other remains unchanged, the equilibrium of the market (equilibrium point) will change. See **equilibrium**, **Fig. 19** (below), **Fig. 42** (p. 109).

Figure 19 Changes in equilibrium caused by increase or decrease in either supply or demand, with other remaining unchanged

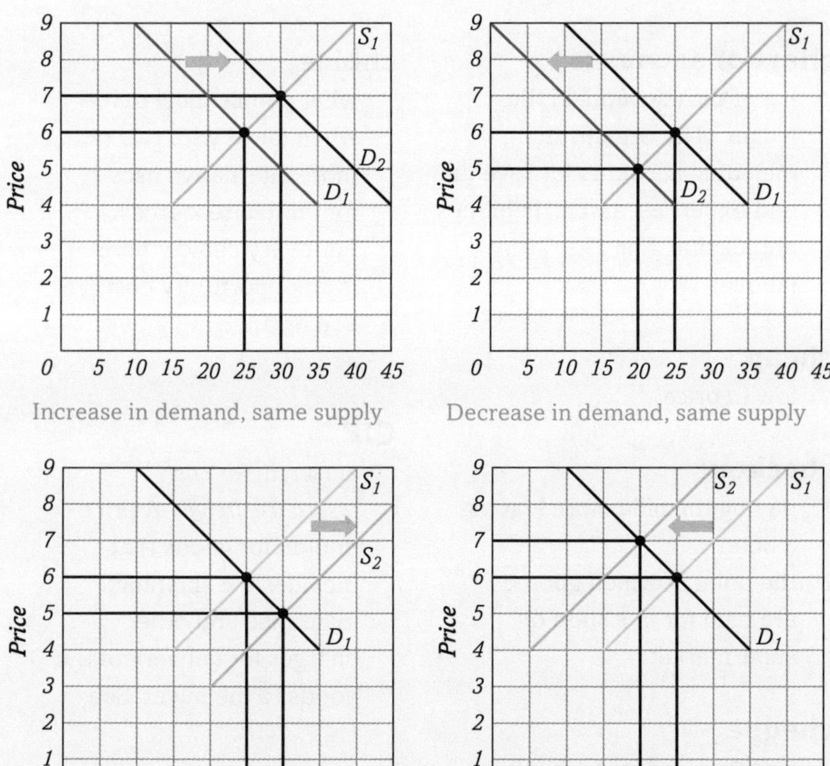

Figure 20 Chart of accounts

No. of Account	Account
100	Sales
200	Opening stock
300	Purchases
400	Closing stock
500	Overhead expenses (detailed)
600	Assets (detailed)
700	Liabilities (detailed)
800	Capital

chart of accounts

list of the accounts in the ledger of an organisation, including accounts for revenue and expenses, assets, liabilities and capital. See **Fig. 20** (above).

cheap

low in price.

checkout

1 paying the bill before leaving a hotel.

2 the point at which goods are paid for in a shop or supermarket.

cheque

a written order to a bank, on a specially printed form, to pay an amount of money from the drawer's account. See **drawer**, **Fig. 21** (p. 53).

choice

what people must make when faced with two or more alternative uses for limited resources. For every choice there is an opportunity cost. See **opportunity cost**, **scarcity**.

CIF

acronym for *cost, insurance, freight*. A price quoted for goods that includes the shipping, insurance and other charges for delivery of the goods to the buyer. See **CAF**, **FOB**.

circular

a letter or advertisement that is distributed to a large number of people.

Figure 21 Cheque

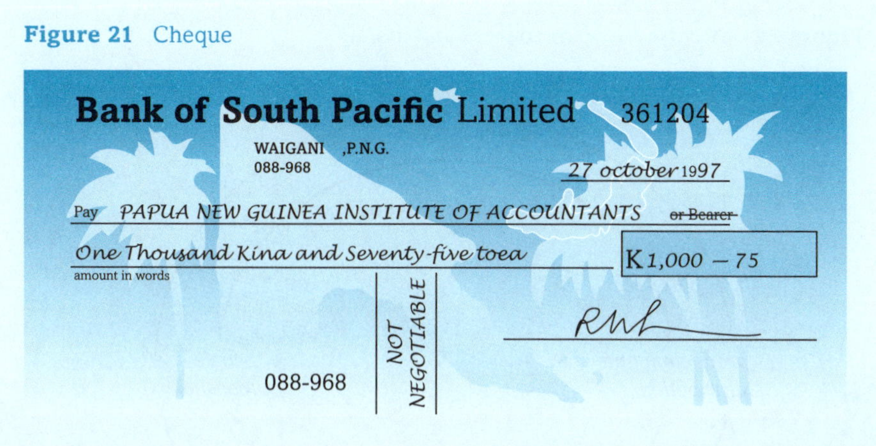
Bank of South Pacific Limited 361204
WAIGANI ,P.N.G.
088-968
27 october 1997
Pay PAPUA NEW GUINEA INSTITUTE OF ACCOUNTANTS ~~or Bearer~~
One Thousand Kina and Seventy-five toea
amount in words
K1,000 – 75
NOT NEGOTIABLE
088-968

circular flow

An economic model that illustrates the flow of goods and services and money though the economy. See Fig. 22 (p. 54).

1 people supply firms with the factors of production (land, labour, capital) and the firms convert these into outputs (goods and services). People consume these goods and services. See **factors of production**.

2 people receive money (wages etc.) from firms for the factors of production and the money then flows back to companies as the people consume and pay for goods and service.

claim

a formal request to an insurance company asking for a payment under the terms of an insurance policy.

claimant

a person making a claim.

classical economics

an approach to economics in which economists believe that markets will react quickly to any changes in equilibrium and therefore governments should not interfere in the market. See **economics**, **Keynesian economics**, **laissez-faire**.

Figure 22 Circular flow of resources and money

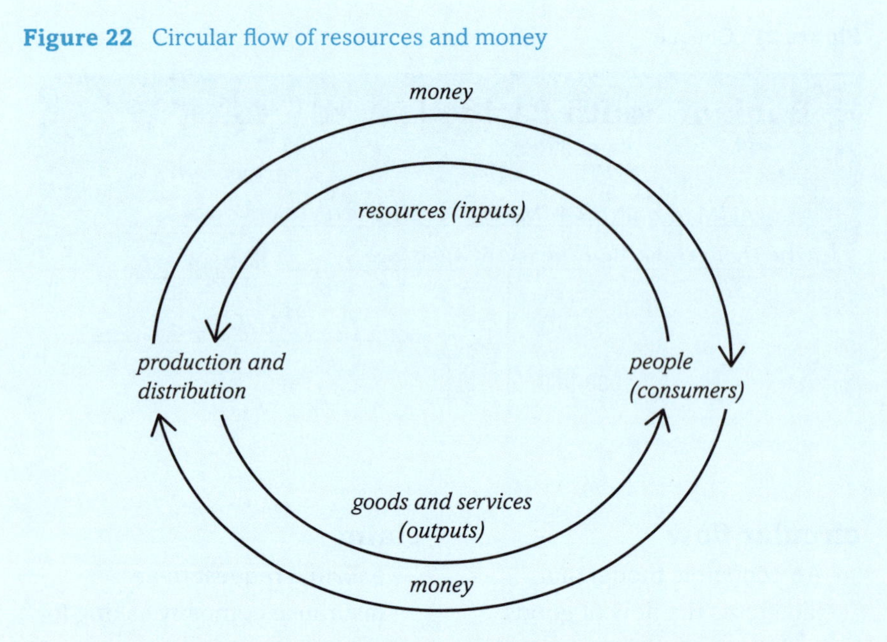

clearance sale

a sale of goods at reduced prices to get rid of unwanted stock or because the shop is closing down.

clearing house

a banking establishment where member banks meet each day, bringing together cheques and commercial papers drawn on each other. The documents are exchanged, their values cancelled against each other and net balances paid in cash. See **clearing system**.

clearing system

a banking process through which cheques and other commercial papers drawn on member banks are settled. See **clearing house**.

clerical staff [**kler**-i-kuhl]

staff of a bank or office who are working as clerks. See **clerk**.

clerk [klahrk]

an employee of a bank or office who processes documents such as invoices and cheques, keeps records and undertakes other administrative duties.

client [**kly**-uhnt]

1 a person who pays a professional person or firm for services.
2 a customer in a shop or hotel.

clientele [kly-uhn-**tel**]

all the clients or customers of a professional person, firm, hotel or shop.

climate change

long-lasting changes in the climate or in the number of extreme weather conditions such as cyclones, floods or droughts. Increased carbon dioxide gas (CO_2) and other greenhouse gases in the atmosphere such as methane produced by human activity are causing global warming, which most scientists believe is causing climate change. The economic effects of climate change for Pacific nations will include:

- decline in agriculture production and increased loss of food security.
- destruction of reef systems with reduction in marine biodiversity and tourism.
- destruction of coastal infrastructure and human settlement by more frequent and extreme storms and flooding.
- social unrest resulting from displacement of people and increased competition for resources.

See **climate**, **climate change adaptation**, **climate change mitigation**, **climate sceptic**, **global warming**, **greenhouse effect**, **greenhouse gas**.

climate change adaptation [ad-ap-**tey**-shn]

policies and actions to overcome the negative economic effects of climate change. Examples include building seawalls and levees to protect property and infrastructure against sea level rise, planting different crops that can survive drought and rising temperatures, and taking extra measures to deal with increased malaria.

climate change mitigation [mit-i-**gay**-shn]
policies and actions to reduce greenhouse emissions. All types of carbon pricing such as carbon offsetting, carbon tax and emissions trading are examples of mitigation against climate change. See **renewable energy**, **carbon pricing**.

climate sceptic [**skep**-tik]
a person who does not believe that the release of CO_2 and other greenhouse gases into the atmosphere by human activity is contributing to global warming and climate change. Climate sceptics believe that climate change is a natural process, and not being caused by the work of humans. See **climate**, **climate change**, **fossil fuel**, **global warming**, **greenhouse effect**, **greenhouse gas**.

closed economy
an economy without contact with the rest of the world. No economies are completely closed, but different countries have different degrees of openness. See **open economy**.

closed shop
a company or place of work that has agreed to employ only union members.

closing-down sale
a sale in which a shop tries to sell all its stock before closing down permanently.

Co.
abbreviation meaning *company*. See **Coy**.

c/o
abbreviation meaning *care of*, which is used in addressing a letter to one person for delivery to another person. For example, when writing to a person who is staying at someone else's home.

COD
acronym for *cash on delivery*. See **cash on delivery**.

coding of accounts
assigning an identification number to each account in the financial statements. A chart

of accounts lists the account titles and account numbers being used by a business. See **chart of accounts**, **Fig. 20** (p. 52).

collateral [kuh-**lat**-er-uhl]
assets used as security for a loan. For example, when a borrower takes out a mortgage, a bank always holds the house as collateral in case of default. See **mortgage**.

collective bargaining
negotiations of wages and other conditions of employment between employers and an organised group of employee such as a union. See **bargaining**, **counter-offer**, **negotiate**.

collective products
See **non-excludable products**.

collusion [kuh-**loo**-zhuhn]
people and companies cooperating or working together when they should be competing. By collaborating with each other, firms try to alter the price of a good to their advantage. Collusion is designed to reduce competition and disrupts market equilibrium. See **anti-competitive practices**, **market equilibrium**, **oligopoly**.

collusive oligopoly [kuh-**loo**-siv ol-i-**gop**-uh-lee]
where members of an oligopoly agree to limit competition between themselves. They may set output quotas, fix prices, limit product promotion or development, or agree not to compete in each other's markets. See **anti-competitive practices**, **collusion**, **oligopoly**.

collusive tendering
where two or more firms secretly agree on the prices they will tender for a contract. These prices will be above those that would be put in under a genuinely competitive tendering process. See **anti-competitive practices**.

command economy
See **centrally planned economy**, **communism**.

commerce

financial transactions, especially the buying and selling of goods or services on a large scale.

commercial

engaged or concerned with commerce.

commercial bank

banks that are mainly concerned with providing consumers with basic cheque and savings accounts, providing small loans to individuals or businesses and sometimes providing home mortgages.

commercial transaction

a business transaction between two parties, in which goods or services are exchanged for payment.

commercialise

[kuh-**mur**-shuh-lyz]

to use something, often sacrificing its pure quality or true meaning, to make money. For example, many businesses commercialise Christmas to make a profit.

commission

an amount paid for the service of buying or selling on behalf of customers. It is usually calculated as a percentage of the value of the transaction, such a real estate agent charging a 5% commission on the sale value of a property.

commissioner for oaths

[kuh-**mish**-uh-ner] [ohthz]

someone who is legally authorised to witness and certify:

- a written statement by someone who needs to say that something is true.
- the validity of certain documents.
- affidavits and depositions (written sworn statements for use as evidence in court).

commodities futures

contracts to buy or sell a given amount of a commodity by a certain date at an agreed price. Futures can be used to reduce risk or speculate on the price movement of an asset. Sellers such as producers of gold or buyers of wheat could use futures to lock in a certain price on a set date and reduce their risk. As in all financial markets, other investors use commodities contracts to gamble on price fluctuations. See **futures contract**, **options**.

commodity [kuh-**mod**-i-tee]

1 in economics, any good produced to satisfy wants and needs.
2 traditionally, a good in which there is little difference between that which comes from one producer or another. For example, a barrel of oil is basically the same product no matter where and who produces it. Other traditional commodities include gold, copper, coffee, copra and natural gas. When they are traded on an exchange, commodities must also meet specified minimum standards, known as a basis grade.
3 more recently, other goods and services such as foreign currency and cell phone minutes have also been classified and traded as commodities.

common law

law based on custom and previous decisions of the courts and not on written laws.

common market

a group of countries that impose few duties on trade with one another and have free movement of labour and capital, common taxes and common trade laws. See **European Union**.

compact disc

See **CD**, **CD-ROM**.

Companies Act

an Act of Parliament that regulates the working of companies and the legal limits within which companies can do business. The Act will differ from country to country.

company

a legally established commercial business, which can be a proprietorship, partnership or corporation. See **corporation**, **limited liability**, **partnership**, **proprietorship**.

company secretary

a senior person who is employed by the board of a company to make sure the decisions of the board are implemented and that the company complies with all legal and regulatory requirements.

comparative advantage

[kuhm-**par**-uh-tiv]

the ability of a company, individual or country to produce goods or services at a lower opportunity cost than other companies, individuals or countries.

compassionate leave

[kuhm-**pash**-uh-nuht]

paid leave given to an employee on the death of a close relative, or for some other personal or family emergency.

compensation

something, usually money, paid to someone to make up for a loss, suffering or injury.

competition

rivalry among sellers to get sales, profit, and market share by offering the best practicable combination of price, quality, and service.

competition laws

law that promotes or maintains market competition by regulating anti-competitive conduct by companies. Competition law is known as antitrust law in the United States and anti-monopoly law in other countries. See **anti-competitive practices**, **collusion**, **collusive oligopoly**, **collusive tendering**, **dividing territories**, **dumping**, **exclusive dealing**, **limit pricing**, **monopoly**, **price fixing**, **refusal to deal**, **resale price maintenance**, **tying**.

competitive advantage

[kuhm-**pet**-i-tiv]

an advantage that a business has over its competitors, allowing it to generate greater sales or margins and have more customers. It can be gained in a variety of ways including cost structure, product quality, distribution network and customer support and loyalty.

competitive equilibrium price [kuhm-**pet**-i-tiv]
the price at which the quantity supplied and the quantity demanded are equal to each other. See **Fig. 42** (p. 109).

competitive pricing
a strategy to capture more of the market by pricing a product in line with, or just below, the prices being charged by competitors.

competitor
a company in the same industry or a similar industry, which offers a similar product or service.

complementary assets [kom-pluh-**men**-tuh-ree]
assets, infrastructure and capabilities that developers of new technologies do not have but need to successfully develop and market their innovations. They have to source these complementary assets source from large existing companies.

complementarity [kom-pluh-men-**tah**-ree-tee]
a relationship between two goods or services, in which a rise in the price of one decreases demand in the other. Complementary goods are used together and are sometimes called complements. Examples of such goods are bottled gas and gas stoves, or cars and fuel. See **cross-elasticity of demand**, **cross-elasticity of supply**, **determinants of demand**, **determinants of supply**.

complementary good [kom-pluh-**men**-tuh-ree]
See **complementarity**.

complements
See **complementarity**.

complementary products
See **complimentarity**.

compliance audit

[kuhm-**ply**-uhns]

a review of financial records to determine whether a firm is following the required rules and regulations.

compounding

See **compound interest**.

compound interest

interest paid on the principal sum of money and also on the accumulated interest of previous periods. See **Fig. 23** (below).

comprehensive motor vehicle insurance

See **motor vehicle insurance**.

compulsory liquidation

[kuhm-**puhl**-suh-ree lik-wi-**dey**-shn]

a situation in which a court orders that a company must stop operating and sell all its assets in order to pay its debts. Also called compulsory winding-up. See **liquidation**.

computer

an electronic device that takes in and stores large amounts of information (data), performs mathematical and other logical functions at high speed and displays the results of these operations. The data is stored in some form of memory, a central processing unit (CPU) uses

Figure 23 Compound interest calculation

Principal invested (in Kina)	1000
10% interest year 1	100
	1100
10% interest year 2	110
	1210
10% interest year 3	121
Repayment of loan and interest	**1331**

programs to process the data and the results are displayed on a television-like visual display unit. See **CPU**, **RAM**, **read-only memory**, **visual display unit (VDU)**.

computer software

a general word for the programs used to operate computers and other similar devices. There are generally two kinds of software programs:

- applications software programs that cause the computer to perform useful activities such as word processing and spreadsheets.
- systems software programs that run the computer and the application software.

concessional loan

a loan with longer repayment terms and lower interest rates than might otherwise be available in the market. Foreign aid to countries from agencies such as the World Bank and the Asian Development Bank are usually in the form of concessional loans. See **foreign aid**, **soft loan**.

consideration

something of value promised to another party when making a contract. The consideration is usually in the form of money, but could be an object or a service.

consignee [kon-sy-**nee**]

1 a person to whom a shipment of goods is delivered. See **air waybill**, **consignment**, **consignor**, **bill of lading**.

2 a person who leaves goods in the possession of another party to sell on their behalf.

consignment
[kuhn-**syn**-muhnt]

1 a batch of goods for delivery to someone. See **air waybill**, **consignee**, **consignor**, **bill of lading**.

2 an arrangement in which the owner of goods leaves them in the possession of another party (the consignor) to sell. Usually the consignor receives a percentage of the sale.

consignor [kon-sy-**nawr**]

1 a person who hands goods over to a carrier for transportation to a consignee; See **air waybill**, **consignee**, **consignment**, **bill of lading**.

2 a person who receives, holds and sells good on behalf of someone else.

consolidated financial statements

statement that brings together all assets, liabilities and operating accounts of a parent company and its subsidiaries. It presents the financial position and results of operations of the parent company and its subsidiaries as if the group were a single company with one or more branches.

consolidation

[kuhn-**sol**-i-dey-tid]

1 the combination of two or more loans into one new loan, usually resulting in a lowering of interest on one or more of the existing loans.

2 the joining two of more corporations into a single entity.

consortium

[kuhn-**sawr**-tee-uhm]

a group made up of two or more individuals, companies or governments who agree to work together towards achieving a specific objective. The members of the consortium remain independent in all business activities other than those relating to their consortium agreement.

constant return to scale

a situation in which outputs increase by the same proportion as the increase in inputs. See **return to scale**.

Constitution

[kon-sti-**tyoo**-shn]

1 a set of basic laws or principles for a country that sets out the rights and duties of its citizens and how it is governed.

2 the basic rules and principles of an organisation, which control how it operates.

consultancy
the professional practice of giving expert advice in a specific field.

consultant
a person providing professional or specialist advice in a specific field.

consumer [kuhn-**syoo**-mer]
a person who buys goods and services to satisfy their own wants and those of their family.

consumer confidence
a measure of how consumers feel about the current and future state of the economy. Generally consumer confidence and spending is high when the unemployment rate is low and GDP growth is high. Consumer spending decreases and saving increases when consumer confidence is low. See **consumer expectations**.

consumer durable
a good bought by a consumer, which is expected to last for a long time. They include private vehicles and domestic goods such as televisions, washing machines and furniture.

consumer expectations
[ek-spek-**tay**-shns]
what consumers anticipate is going to happen in the market. This includes what consumers think is going to happen to prices, the economy and their own income. Consumer expectations affect demand.

For example, if consumers think that the price of rice will go up because of shipping problems, they may immediately buy more rice. On the other hand, if customers believe that the price of a computer will decrease when a new model comes out, they may decide to wait for a while before making a purchase.

consumer good
goods that are designed for final used by consumers.

consumer income
disposable or household income that is the amount of income remaining after taxes and living expenses

have been deducted. Increase in consumer income usually results in an increase in demand for what are called normal goods. The demand for some goods, however, can decrease when consumer income rises. These goods are called inferior goods. See **inferior good**, **normal goods**.

consumerism

[kuhn-**syoo**-muh-riz-uhm]

1 the protection or promotion of consumers' interests in relation to the producer, such as improvements in safety standards and truthful packaging and advertising. Also called consumer protection.

2 the preoccupation of society with the acquisition of consumer goods and the belief that the more materials acquired the better. Sometimes referred to as greed.

consumer price index (CPI)

the average cost of a fixed basket of goods and services that can be compared with the cost of the same basket of goods and services at some previous time (called the base period). The cost at the base period is assigned the value 100. Fig. 24 (p. 67) is a graph of the CPI for Papua New Guinea that was published by the World Bank in 2013. In this case the year 2004 is used as the base period. See **base period**, **basket**, **deflation**, **inflation**, **inflation rate**, **Fig. 24** (p. 67).

consumer protection

See **consumerism**.

consumer research

investigation of consumers' needs and preferences, especially in relation to a particular product or service.

consumer sovereignty

[**sov**-rin-tee]

the situation in an economy where the needs and wants of consumers control the output of producers.

consumer spending

the purchase of consumer goods and services.

Figure 24 Consumer Price Index – Papua New Guinea (base period 2004)

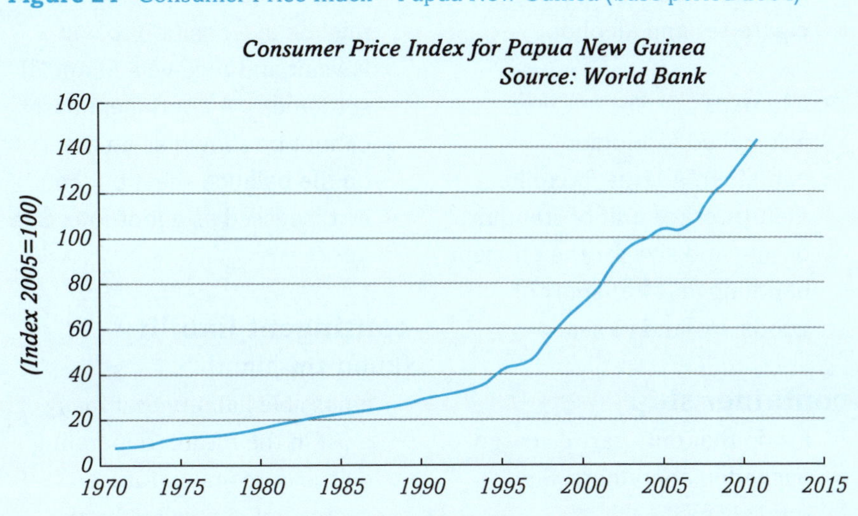

consumer surplus

the money gained by a consumer who was able to buy a good or a service for less than they were willing to pay.

consumer taste and preference [**pref**-er-uhns]

the changing likes and dislikes of consumers for goods affect demand. Young peoples' choice of clothes and music, for example, are continually changing, resulting in changes in demand.

consumption [kuhn-**suhmp**-shn]

the using up of goods and services to satisfy wants and needs.

consumption expenditure

the total expenditure on all goods and services to satisfy the wants and needs of a household.

consumption goods

goods that are bought by households to use up, such

as bus tickets, food, clothing, cigarettes and alcohol.

container

also called a shipping container. A large, box-like, metal storage unit of standard design and size for the efficient handling and transport of goods, by land or sea.

container ship

a ship that only carries cargo packed in containers. See **container**.

contingency plan
[kuhn-**tin**-juhn-see]

a plan that lays out a course of action a business will take in response to a future event. For example, a company might have plans to move its operations to a different location if a fire, flood, cyclone or earthquake made it impossible to continue in its current location.

contingent asset
[kuhn-**tin**-juhnt]

an asset in which the possible economic benefit depends on the outcome of future events not controlled by the company. For example, a company may be in a position to win a lawsuit and receive a financial settlement. A contingent asset cannot be shown as an asset on the balance sheet but can be discussed as a footnote. See **asset**.

contingent liability
[kuhn-**tin**-juhnt]

a possible liability that may exist in the future, depending on the outcome of future events not controlled by the company. Examples include an adverse decision in court regarding tax, or a lawsuit. An estimate of the potential liability should be included as a footnote to the balance sheet. See **liability**.

contraband

goods that have been imported or exported illegally.

contract

a written or spoken agreement between two or more people, companies or countries that has been entered into voluntarily and is enforceable by law. Contracts are mostly associated with the exchange of goods and services, money and properties.

contraction

a period during which the economy as a whole is in decline. A contraction in the economy can cause hardship for most people as people start losing their jobs. While no economic contraction lasts forever, a contraction can last for many years, such as the Great Depression of the 1930s.

contract law

the laws that govern written or spoken agreements (contracts) between two or more people, companies or countries.

contract of employment

a legal agreement between employer and employee. An employment contract would normally contain information about matters such as salary, benefits and length of employment.

contractor

1 the person or company who has agreed to provide goods or services under the terms of a contract.

2 a business offering a service, such as a garbage removal contractor.

cook the books

to record false information in the accounts of an organisation in order to hide losses or steal money. See **creative accounting**.

cooperative

a society or business that is owned and run by its members. The members share the profits among themselves.

co-opt

appoint to membership of a committee or other body by an invitation from the existing members.

copyright

exclusive and legal right given to an author or artist to print, publish, perform, film, or record literary, artistic or musical material. No other person is legally allowed to make copies without the copyright holder's permission.

corporate culture

values, beliefs and behaviour deliberately created by a company. A company's corporate culture determines how its employees and management interact with each other and with customers, investors and the greater community.

corporate social responsibility (CSR)

a belief that a company should be socially, ethically and environmentally responsible for its actions. CSR requires that the responsibility of business is more than just its legal responsibility to its shareholders to achieve maximum profit.

corporate tax

also called corporation tax or company tax. Taxes paid against profits earned by a business during a given period of time. Corporate tax rates and laws vary greatly around the Pacific region.

corporate welfare

when a government gives a business money or monetary benefits such as tax cuts and subsidies. For example, a government may help a business that employs many local people, in order to keep it from moving to a new location or closing down.

corporation

a legally formed entity that is separate from its owners or shareholders. The most important aspect of a corporation is limited liability. That is, shareholders have the right to participate in the profits, through dividends and/ or the appreciation of stock, but are not held personally liable for the company's debts. See **entity**, **limited liability**.

cost

price paid to acquire, produce or maintain goods or services. Prices paid for materials, labour and factory overheads in the manufacture of goods and for their delivery and marketing are costs. See **fixed costs**, **total costs**, **variable costs**.

cost accountant

an accountant who is concerned with the costing system in a business. Also referred to as a management accountant.

cost and freight

See **CAF**.

cost–benefit analysis (CBA)

a comparison of the cost of a business activity with the resulting benefits in order to decide whether or not it should go ahead.

cost curve

a graph of total costs of production (fixed costs plus variable costs) as a function of total quantity of units produced. See **total cost**, **fixed costs**, **variable costs**, **Fig. 25** (below).

cost-effective

describing the relationship between money spent and the desired outputs. For example, an advertising campaign that results in an increase in sales

Figure 25 Total cost

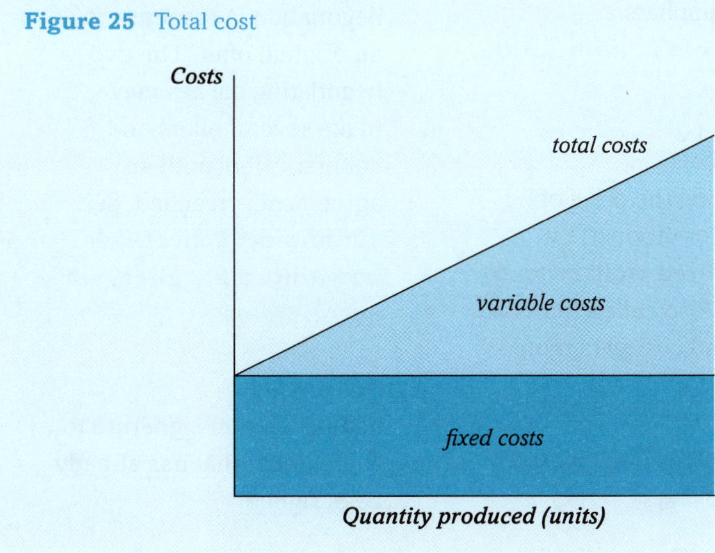

revenue greater than the cost of the advertising is said to have been cost-effective.

cost insurance and freight

See **CIF**.

cost minimisation

achieving the cheapest way of delivering goods and services to the required level of quality. Strategies to minimise costs include:

- eliminating waste.
- simplifying processes.
- outsourcing non-core activities such as call handling.
- negotiating better prices with suppliers.
- See **profit maximisation**.

cost plus

a method of determining the price of a service or product, by adding a fixed profit factor to the cost. Also called full-cost pricing and cost plus profit pricing.

cost plus profit pricing

See **cost plus**.

cost-push inflation

inflation caused by increases in the cost of wages and raw materials. The higher costs of production are passed on to consumers in the form of higher prices. See **inflation**.

cost price

the price that it costs to purchase or produce a good, with no profit added on.

counterfeit [**kown**-ter-fit]

a forged or illegal imitation of something. Often refers to forged bank notes.

counter-offer

an offer made during a negotiation in response to an original offer. The two negotiating parties may make several offers and counter-offers until an agreement is reached. See **bargaining**, **collective bargaining**, **haggling**, **wage negotiations**.

countersign

adding another signature to a document that has already been signed.

covenant [**kuhv**-uh-nuhnt]

an agreement or contract between two or more parties, in which one or both parties agree to do, or not do, certain specified actions. Loans from the International Monetary Fund and the World Bank often require the borrowing country to undertake actions such as privatisation and reducing corruption and the size of the public service.

Coy

abbreviation meaning *company*. See **Co**.

CPI

see **consumer price index**.

CPU

acronym for the *central processing unit* of a computer, where the processing of all of the data takes place. The CPU is the 'brain' of the computer and is sometimes called the *processor*.

cr

abbreviation for *credit*.

creative accounting

where the accounts have been presented in a way that makes the company's financial position seem better that it really is. See **cook the books**.

credit

1. the action of recording an amount on the credit side of the ledger.
2. the right-hand column of an account.
3. an arrangement to obtain goods and services before paying, based on the seller's trust that payment will be made in the future.

credit balance

1. in accounting, when the value of the credit side of the ledger is larger than the value of the debit side.
2. an amount of money in a bank account.

credit card

a plastic card issued by a bank or other financial company, which allows the holder to buy goods and services on credit, or obtain money on loan. Credit cards charge interest

Figure 26 A credit card

and are usually used for short-term financing. Interest charges normally begin one month after a purchase is made and borrowing limits are pre-set according to the individual's credit rating. See **credit rating**, **Fig. 26** (above).

credit control

an activity that:

1. increases sales revenue by extending credit to customers who are trusted and considered a good credit risk.
2. reduces risk of loss from bad debts by restricting or denying credit to customers who are considered to be not a good credit risk.

credit note

a receipt given by a seller to a customer when goods are returned by a customer or an overcharge has been made. The seller then either refunds the money to the customer or deducts that amount from the customer's next purchase.

credit rating

an estimate of the ability of a person, organisation or country to repay debts. The rating is based on previous experience and is used by banks and businesses to determine the amount of credit they will give. See **credit risk**.

credit risk

the risk that a borrower will default on any type of debt by failing to make the required payments. See **credit control**, **credit rating**.

credit sale

a sale of goods and services for which the consumer is not required to make full payment at the time of purchase. The seller trusts that payment will be made in the future.

creditor

a person or company to whom money is owed.

criteria

standards or measures that people use to evaluate what is best or most important when making choices between alternatives. See **alternatives**, **choice**.

cross-elasticity of demand [ih-la-**stis**-i-tee]

a measure of the change in demand for one good when a change in price takes place for another good.

Cross-elasticity of demand is negative for complementary goods, positive for substitute goods and zero for goods that are not related. For example, if a 10% increase in the price of fuel decreases the demand for cars by 20%, the cross-elasticity of demand is:

$$= -\frac{20\%}{10\%} = -2$$

See **complementary goods**, **elasticity**, **normal goods**, **substitute goods**, **Fig. 27** (below).

Figure 27 Cross-elasticity of demand

$$E_{A,B} = \frac{\text{\% change in the quantity demanded of product A}}{\text{\% change in the price of product B}}$$

Figure 28 Cross-elasticity of supply

$$E_{A, B} = \frac{\text{\% change in the quantity supplied of product A}}{\text{\% change in the price of product B}}$$

cross-elasticity of supply

a measure of a change in the quantity supply of one good when a change in price takes place for another good. Cross-elasticity of supply is positive for complementary goods, negative for substitute goods and zero for goods that are not related. For example, if a 10% increase in the price of English potatoes decreases the supply of sweet potatoes by 10%, the cross-elasticity of demand is:

$$= \frac{+10\%}{-10\%} = -1$$

See **complementary goods**, **elasticity**, **normal goods**, **substitute goods**, **Fig. 28** (above).

crossed cheque

a cheque that has two lines drawn across it to show that it can only be paid into a bank account and not exchanged for cash. See **account payee only**, **cheque**.

crowding in

an economic theory stating that increased government expenditure increases the demand for goods and services that are provided to government by business, leading to higher private-sector investment. See **crowding out**.

crowding out

an economic theory stating that increased government expenditure reduces or replaces investment by business. This can happen in two ways:

- when governments borrow large amounts of capital to fund public-sector expenditure, interest rates can rise, thus discouraging business from borrowing money and thereby reducing investment.
- when government provides a service or good that would otherwise be a

business opportunity for private industry, it competes with business or crowds business out of the market.

See **crowding in**.

cumulative dividend [**kyoo**-myuh-ley-tiv]

see **dividend**.

currency [**kuhr**-en-see]

the money in general use in a country.

currency appreciation

an increase in the value of one currency in terms of another. When a currency appreciates, one unit will buy more units of another currency. Currencies can appreciate or depreciate in value against each other.

currency union

where two or more countries share the same currency. See **euro**.

current account

The sum of the following:

- the difference between the value of exported and imported goods and services.
- the difference between the receipts from income-generating investments made abroad and those earned by foreign in-country investors.
- the difference between remittances made by citizens working overseas and cash sent home by foreign workers in the country.
- the difference between money received as grants, gifts and aid from foreign countries and grants, gifts and aid given to other countries

See **balance of payments**, **capital account**.

current assets

a company's assets in a balance sheet that include all assets that are expected to be converted into cash within a year of the date of the balance sheet. Current assets include cash, accounts receivable, stock (inventory), marketable securities and prepaid expenses. See **non-current assets**.

current liabilities
a company's debts or obligations as shown in the balance sheet that are due to be paid within a year of the date of the balance sheet. See **non-current liabilities**.

curriculum vitae [kuh-**rik**-yuh-luhm **vee**-ty]
a summary of a person's education, qualifications and work history and experience, usually sent when applying for a job. Also known as a c.v.

custodian
[kuh-**stoh**-dee-uhn]
a person who has the responsibility of taking care or protecting property or records. Traditional custodians of land and sea are an important aspect of many Pacific cultures.

customary land
See **custodians**, **land ownership in Melanesia**.

customary law
the accepted behaviour and standards that have been long established in a local community. It is the law according to custom and an important aspect of many Pacific cultures.

custom-built
something that has been made or built according to the specifications of a customer.

customer
an individual or business that purchases goods or services from another business.

customise
to modify something according to a customer's individual requirements.

customs
the government department authorised to administer and collect duties levied by a government on imported goods.

customs duty
the tax levied by a government on imported goods to raise

revenue and/or to protect domestic industries.

c.v.
See **curriculum vitae**.

cyclical employment
[**sik**-li-kuhl]
See **cyclical unemployment**.

cyclical unemployment
workers losing their jobs due to fluctuations in output caused by changes in the economy as it cycles through booms and recessions. See **frictional unemployment**, **structural unemployment**, **Fig. 29** (below).

Figure 29 *Cyclical unemployment compared to growth in real GDP*

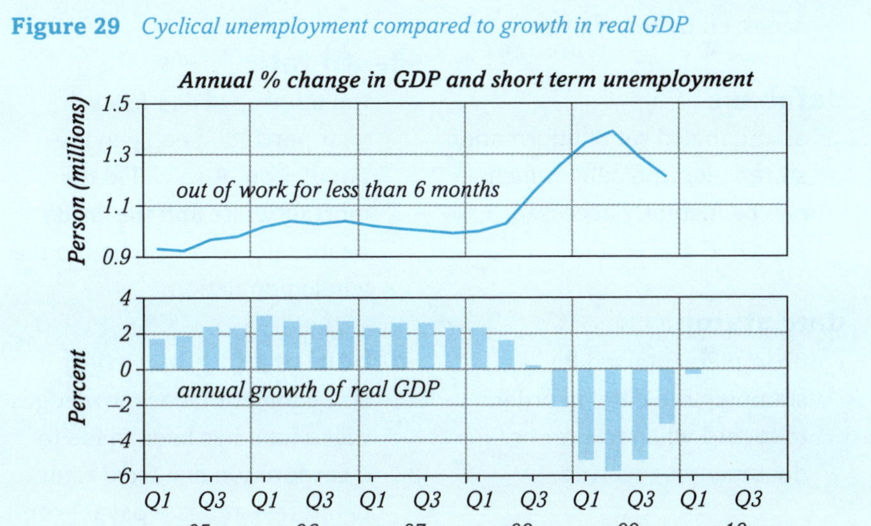

data [**day**-ta or **dah**-ta]

a collection of information.

databank

a large collection of computer data, often from more than one database, which can be accessed by many users.

database

an organised set of information stored electronically, which can be instantly accessed, searched and sorted.

date stamp

an implement used for stamping the date, in order to record when a letter or document is received.

deadline

the final day by which an agreed action must be taken.

deal

a business agreement to buy or sell goods or provide a service.

dealer

- a person who buys and sells goods and services.
- a person or company that buys and sells its own securities, usually through a broker. See **security**.

death rate

the number of deaths each year per 1000 people in the population. Also called the mortality rate and the crude death rate, when applied to the whole population.

debenture [dih-**ben**-cher]

a document that acknowledges that a loan has been made to a corporation at a fixed rate of interest and is repayable on a fixed date. Debentures are usually freely traded.

debit

1 the action of recording an amount of money owed on the debit side of the ledger.

Figure 30 Debt–equity ratio

$$\text{Debt} - \text{equity ratio} = \frac{\text{Total liabilities}}{\text{Stockholder equity}}$$

2 the left-hand column of an account.
3 removal of money by a bank from a customer's account

debit balance

1 when the debit side of the ledger is larger than the credit side.
2 the amount owed by an account holder to the bank when an account is overdrawn.

debit card

a card that allows the holder to electronically transfer money out of their bank account when making a purchase or withdrawing cash at an ATM. See **automatic teller machine (ATM)**, **credit card**.

debt [det]

an amount of money borrowed by one party from another. Companies and individuals use debt as a method for making purchases they cannot afford to pay for immediately.

debt collector [det]

a company or individual whose business is the recovery of overdue debts. Hired by companies to which money is owed by debtors, debt collectors operate for a fee or for a percentage of the total amount collected.

debt–equity ratio [det **ek**-wi-tee **rey**-shee-oh]

the ratio of the total liabilities of a business to its shareholder equity. See **equity**, **liability**, **Fig. 30** (above).

debtor [**det**-er]

a person or organisation who owes money to another person or organisation.

debt servicing

paying the interest and capital repayments on debt.

debt–service ratio

a measure of the level of debt of an individual or country. For a family it is the ratio of total debt repayments to gross family income. For a country it is the ratio of total debt-servicing payments to export earnings.

debug

to identify and remove errors from computer hardware and software.

decision making

the process of making a choice after the evaluation of all available options. See **alternatives**, **choice**, **criteria**.

deed

a signed legal document, usually referring to ownership of property or legal rights.

deed of partnership

a legal document setting out the legal rights and responsibilities of partners.

default

1 failure of a debtor to meet principal or interest payments on a debt at the due date.

2 failure or refusal of a sovereign state to meet its international debt obligations.

defendant

a person or company sued or accused in a court of law.

deferred expenditure

[dih-**furd**]

expenses that have been incurred but do not apply to the current accounting period. An example is an advance payment such as an annual insurance policy that extends for a period of time greater than the current accounting period. The amount covering the period outside the accounting period is recorded as an asset until such time as it is used.

deferred income

advance payments or cash received before the goods or services have been supplied. This income is recorded on the recipient's balance sheet as a liability, until the goods or services have been supplied.

deficit [**de**-fis-it]

an amount by which expenses are greater than income.

deficit spending
government spending that is in excess of government revenues. Deficit spending uses funds that have been borrowed.

deflation [dih-**fley**-shn]
a decrease in the general price of goods and services, as indicated by a fall in the CPI. Deflation is said to be occurring when the inflation rate falls below 0% (a negative inflation rate). Between July and September 2007, the inflation rate in PNG was –1.61%. See **CPI**, **inflation**, **inflation rate**.

deflationary policy
fiscal or monetary policy of a country, designed to reduce the rate of growth of aggregate demand. See **aggregate demand**.

deindustrialisation [dee-in-**duhs**-tree-uh-ly-zay-shn]
a decrease over time of the manufacturing sector, usually accompanied by a growth in the service sector and an increase in the import of manufactured goods. See **industrialisation**.

delegation [del-i-**gay**-shn]
1 the assignment of authority and responsibility, normally by a manager to a subordinate or another person, to carry out specific activities.
2 a group of people sent to represent a company or country at a conference or convention.

delivery
to bring or transport letters, messages, goods, etc. to the place or recipient to whom they are addressed.

delivery note
a document sent with a shipment of goods that lists the description and quantity of goods being delivered.

delivery price
1 the price quoted for a good that includes freight charges for delivery to the buyer.
2 the price agreed to deliver and accept the commodity referred to in a futures contract or a stock's selling price in an

options contract. See **futures contract**, **option**.

demand

the different quantities of a good consumers are willing and able to buy at each of a range of prices at a specific period of time. See **demand curve**, **demand schedule** and **Fig. 32** (p. 85).

demand curve

a graph of a demand schedule, showing the relationship between the quantity of a good that good consumers will buy at each of different prices. The demand curve is usually a straight line sloping downwards, showing that demand increases as the price decreases. Other factors affecting demand include consumer income and the price of other goods. The demand curve will shift if any of these factors change. See **demand schedule**, **determinants of demand**, **elasticity**, **Fig. 19** (p. 51), **Fig. 31a** and **31b** (p. 85).

demand determinants

[dih-**tur**-muh-nuhntz]

See **determinants of demand**.

demand elasticity

See **elasticity of demand**.

demand-deficient unemployment

See **cyclical unemployment**.

demand inflation

inflation caused by excessive consumer demand. When aggregate demand is greater than aggregate supply, prices will rise, causing inflation. See **cost inflation**, **demand-side policy**.

demand-pull inflation

See **demand inflation**.

demand schedule

[**shed**-yool]

a table showing the quantity demanded of a good or service for each of different prices at given period of time, all other things being equal. See **demand curve**, **supply schedule**, **Fig. 31a** (p. 85), **Fig. 32** (p. 85) and **Fig. 64** (p. 246).

Figure 31a Demand curve

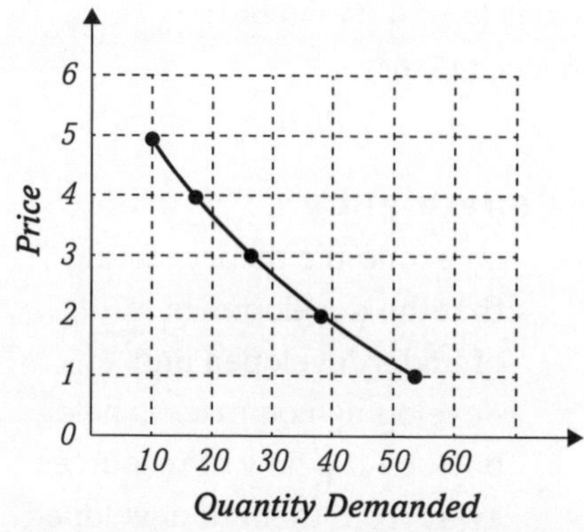

Figure 31b Demand curve shift with increased income

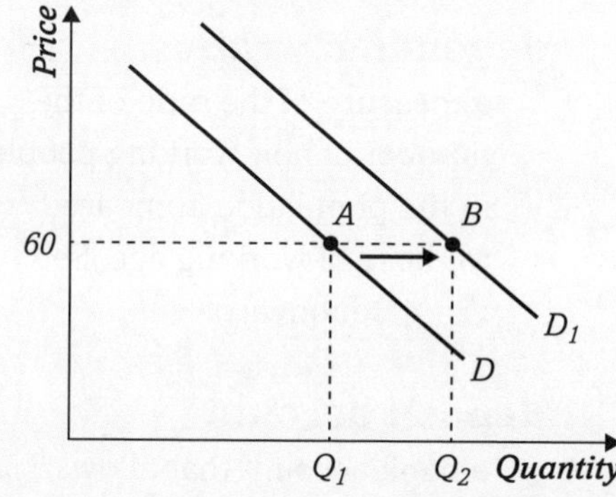

Figure 32 Demand schedule

Demand schedule for fresh fish, one day	
Price per kg (Kina)	Quantity demanded (kg)
1.00	200
1.50	150
2.00	100
2.50	50

demand-side policy

government policies designed to increase aggregate demand in the economy. They include such strategies as lowering interest rates and tax rates in order to increase the money that people have to spend. Demand-side policies are useful for short-term economic

Figure 33 Dependency ratio

$$\text{Dependency ratio} = \frac{\text{Number of dependants (aged 0–14 and 65+)}}{\text{Number of workers (aged 15–64)}} \times 100\%$$

growth but carry the danger of causing inflation. See **demand inflation**, **supply-side policy**.

demerit good

good or service that does harm, such as alcohol, tobacco and gambling.

demurrage [dih-**mur**-ij]

a charge payable to a ship owner by a charterer (hirer) of the ship, for not loading or unloading the ship within the agreed time.

dependants' rebate

a tax deduction given to an income-earner who is looking after close relatives. The rebate is deducted from the normal tax payable in order to calculate the actual tax payable. In some countries, dependants' rebates are allowable for spouses who do not work, and for children.

dependency

an economic theory stating that the development of underdeveloped and developing countries is held back by the flow of resources away from them to developed countries.

dependency ratio

a measure of the ratio of the number of non-working people in the population compared to those of working age. See **Fig. 33** (above).

deposit account

a bank account that allows money to be deposited and withdrawn by the account holder. Some banks charge a fee for their service, while others may pay the customer interest on the account balance.

deposit slip

the document used to record details of moneys being paid

by a customer into their bank account.

depreciation

[dih-pree-shee-**ay**-shn]

1 for accounting purposes, depreciation represents how much of the value of an asset used in production has been used up. For example, a company may buy a piece of equipment costing K1 million, which is expected to have a useful life of 10 years. The company can, using straight-line depreciation, write off to expenses K100 000 each accounting year. See **amortise**, **diminishing value**, **reducing balance**, **straight-line depreciation**, **write off**.

2 for tax purposes, a business can annually depreciate or deduct as a business expense a proportion of the cost of a tangible asset. How and when such deductions can be made are governed by the country's taxation rules.

3 currencies and real estate can also lose value or depreciate.

depreciation tax allowance

the amount by which, based on the depreciation of tangible assets, a business can reduce its profit when taxes are calculated. This amount may be different from the amount of depreciation written off in the profit and loss account and is governed by the country's taxation rules and regulations. See **profit and loss account**.

deregulation

[dee-reg-yuh-**lay**-shn]

the reduction or complete removal of government power in an industry, thus creating more competition within the industry. The telephone, power and water industries in many Pacific countries are being deregulated to eliminate government monopoly and open the market to private firms.

derivative [dih-**riv**-uh-tiv]

contracts such as futures, options and swaps in which the investor does not own the good but can sell it. Examples of derivatives that can be bought and sold include:

- contracts in which one party agrees to sell a good and another party (the investor) agrees to buy the good at a specific price on a specific date. The buyer hopes the value of the good will increase so that they can make a profit, while the seller is protected from a possible drop in the value of the good.
- debts such as when a bank that has provided loans to customers sells the loans to an investor at a discounted rate. The bank receives its money to undertake other business and the buyer hopes to make a profit on the interest received from the loans or by on-selling the debt to another investor.
- a person with a fixed-interest loan swaps the loan with someone who has a variable-interest loan. One hopes the interest rate will fall, while the other hopes it will rise.

See **futures**, **options contract**.

derived demand

the demand for one good or service resulting from a change in price of a related good or service. See **complementary goods**.

detriment good

[**de**-truh-muhnt]

good or service that does harm, such as alcohol, tobacco and gambling.

determinants of demand

factors that determine demand. Price is one of these factors. Others include the price of other goods (especially substitute and complementary goods), consumers' income, the number of consumers in the market and their tastes and preferences. See **complementary goods**, **consumer expectations**, **consumer income**, **consumer tastes and preferences**, **demand curve**, **substitute goods**.

determinants of supply

factors that determine supply. Price is one of these factors. Others include the price of other goods (especially substitute and complementary goods), costs of production, number of suppliers in the market, availability of resources and the weather. See **complementary good**, **substitute good**.

detriment good

[**de**-truh-muhnt]

See **demerit good**.

devaluation

[dee-val-yoo-**ay**-shn]

an official reduction in the value of the currency of a country, relative to other currencies. Devaluation causes a country's exports to become less expensive, making them more competitive on the global market. But imports become *more* expensive, driving domestic consumers' demand for them.

developed economy (country)

a country that has a high level of economic growth. General characteristics of a developed economy include widespread infrastructure, a relatively high per-capita income or gross domestic product (GDP), industrialisation and a high standard of living. Examples of developed countries include the United States of America, Canada, most of western Europe, Australia, Japan and New Zealand. See **gross domestic product**, **gross domestic product per capita**, **human development index**, **Fig. 47** (p. 133), **Fig. 48** (p. 138).

developing economy (country)

a general term used to describe all countries that have not yet achieved the high level of economic development needed to be considered developed. However, the economic situation in these countries is not all the same:

- Some have advanced and developed economies but have not yet achieved all the characteristics of a developed economy. Examples include Brazil, Russia, India and China.
- Some have economies with the potential of being strong emerging economies in the 21st century. Examples include Indonesia, Iran, Nigeria and Vietnam.

- Some have an inconsistent record of economic development. (These make up 76% of the world's countries.)

Some are in sharp economic decline. See **failed state.**

diminishing marginal returns [dih-**min**-ish-ing **mahr**-juh-nl]

See **diminishing returns – theory of**.

diminishing returns

See **diminishing returns – theory of**.

diminishing returns – theory of

a theory stating that if one input of production (such as the number of workers) is increased while all other inputs (such as the number of machines or workspaces) remains unchanged, there will come a point where the marginal (additional) output per additional unit of input (in this case worker) will start to decrease. See **marginal physical product (MPP)**.

diminishing returns to scale

See **returns to scale**.

diminishing value

a method of calculating the depreciation of an asset. Annual depreciation is calculated on the reducing value of the asset. For example, a 10% depreciation on an asset bought for K1000 would be 10% of K1000 = K100 in the first year. In the second year, the depreciation is calculated on the reduced value of the asset: 10% of K900 (K1000 – K100) and so on each following year. Also known as the reducing-balance method of depreciation.

direct costs

costs related directly to the production of a good or service, such as materials and labour. See **indirect costs**.

direct debit

an amount of money taken out of an account by the bank, on the instruction of the account holder. It is usually credited to the account of another person or organisation to whom the amount is owed.

direct inward investment

an external or foreign company either investing in or purchasing the goods of a local economy. Inward investment creates jobs and brings wealth into the economy.

direct tax

a tax, such as income tax, that is paid straight to the government.

director

a member of a company's board of directors, appointed by the shareholders. Directors are responsible for the overall management of the company. See **board of directors**, **managing director**.

dirty floating

See **managed floating exchange rate**.

disc

a circular, plastic, optical data-storage device, designed for recording, storing and playing back audio, video and computer data. Pronounced the same as *disk*, the 'c' spelling is used for optical storage devices while the 'k' spelling is used for magnetic storage devices. See **CD**, **disk**.

discount

an amount taken off the regular price of a good or service, usually for payment in cash or payment within a required date. See **trade discount**.

discount rate

the percentage rate used by banks when discounting bills of exchange.

discounted bill of exchange

a bill of exchange sold to a bank before the due date, at a reduced amount. The holder of the bill obtains cash (less than the value of the bill) earlier than expected, while the bank holds on to the bill and obtains full value when payment comes due. See **bill of exchange**, **Fig. 14** (p. 30), **Fig. 54** (p. 181).

discounted cash flow

a method of valuing an investment by discounting cash flows (returns) to give them a present day value. The sum of all future cash flows is called the *net present value*. See **net present value**.

diseconomies of scale

where the average cost of production per unit increase as the scale of production increases beyond a certain point. See **economies of sale.**

disguised unemployment [dis-**gyzd**]

when more people than required are employed to undertake an activity. Disguised unemployment is often found in developing countries whose large populations create a surplus in the labour force. Where more people are employed than is necessary, the overall productivity of each individual decreases.

dishonour [dis-**on**-er]

when a bank refuses to pay a cheque or bill of exchange because there is not enough money in the account on which it was drawn. See **dishonoured cheque**.

dishonoured cheque

a cheque that a bank refuses to pay because there is not enough money in the account on which it was drawn. Sometimes called a bounced cheque. See **bounced cheque**, **refer to drawer**, **represent**.

disk

a thin, circular sheet of magnetic material, used to store digital computer information. Information can be read from the disk or written onto the disk by a computer. Pronounced the same as disc, the ‘k’ spelling is used for magnetic storage devices while the ‘c’ spelling is used for optical storage devices. See **CD**, **disc**, **hard disk**, **hard drive**.

disk drive

See **hard drive**.

disposable income

[dih-**spoh**-zuh-buhl]

the amount of money that a household has available for spending and saving after income taxes and other deductions have been paid.

distribution

1 the process of moving goods and services from producers to the final consumers.

2 the way in which something is shared out among a group or spread over an area.

disutility

The negative or harmful effects of an activity or the consumption of a good, particularly over a long period of time.

diversification

[dy-vur-suh-fi-**kay**-shn]

when a company expands into new types of business.

dividend

a sum of money paid to shareholders out of the profits of the company. There are different types of dividends:

- *cumulative dividend (cum div)*: the sale price of the share plus the next dividend to be declared but not yet paid.
- *ex dividend (ex div)*: the sale price of the share without inclusion of any dividends.
- *final dividend*: the dividend that will be paid at the end of the financial year.
- *interim dividend*: a dividend paid as part of the annual dividend, paid half-way through the year.
- *dividend cover*: the number of times the profit after tax covers the dividend paid for the year. Includes the interim plus final dividend. For example, if the profits after tax are K10 000 and the dividend paid is K5000, the dividend is covered twice.
- *dividend per share*: the amount of money paid as dividend for each share held. For example, if the dividend paid is K25 000 and there are 50 000 shares, then the dividend is 50 toea per share.
- *dividend withholding tax*: the amount of tax deducted from the dividend paid by the company. It is part

of the tax payable by shareholders on dividends received.

- *dividend yield*: the ratio of the dividend received to the price of the share, expressed as a percentage.

dividend cover

see **dividend**.

dividend per share

see **dividend**.

dividend withholding tax

see **dividend**.

dividend yield

see **dividend**.

dividing territories

an agreement between two companies to each operate in an agreed area, to stay out of each other's way and reduce competition. See **anti-competitive practices**.

division of labour

a system in which different members of a society do different types of work. This allows individuals to specialise in types of work in which they have a competitive advantage and to develop specialised skills through training and experience.

document

a written record of an event or agreement.

Doha Round

the latest round of trade negotiations among the World Trade Organization (WTO) membership. Beginning in 2001, the round continues with regular ministerial-level meetings. Its aim is to lower trade barriers and increase global trade. See **General Agreement on Tariffs and Trade (GATT)**, **Uruguay Round**, **World Trade Organization (WTO)**.

domestic product

the value of the total production of goods and services in a country, by both locally owned and foreign-owned enterprises. See **gross domestic product (GDP)**.

double entry bookkeeping

a system of accounting in which every payment appears

twice in different accounts, once as a credit and once as a debit. The system provides a check on accuracy and is the basis of properly kept financial records.

double time
twice the normal rate of pay for working overtime in accordance with terms and conditions of service, or the worker's award.

doubtful debts
debts that might not be paid. An allowance as a loss is made for them in the profit and loss account. When they are actually written off, they become bad debts.

down payment
a partial payment made at the time of purchase, with the balance to be paid later.

down streaming
See **forward integration**.

downward-sloping demand curve
the normal slope of a demand curve, showing that the quantity demanded decreases as the price increases. See **demand curve**.

drawee
the bank in which the account of a person writing a cheque is held.

drawer
the person who signs the cheque.

drawings
when a sole trader or a partner in a partnership draws money from the business. The amount is referred to and accounted for as drawings.

drip pricing
when a company advertises a low price for its product or service, and only later in the purchase process do consumers learn that there are additional surcharges or add-on fees. Drip pricing is particularly common on online shopping sites.

dumping
where a company sells a product in a competitive market at a loss. Though the

company loses money on each sale, it hopes to force other competitors out of the market, after which the company would be free to raise prices for a greater profit. See **anti-competitive practices**.

duopoly [dyoo-**op**-uh-lee]
an oligopoly where there are just two firms in the market. See **monopoly**, **oligopoly**.

duplicate
a second copy of a document such as an invoice or credit note.

durable consumer good
See **consumer durables**, **consumer good**.

duty-free goods
goods that can be imported without customs duty being paid on them.

E and OE

acronym for *errors and omissions excepted.* Placed at the end of an invoice, it shows that the firm takes no responsibility for clerical mistakes and allows the supplier to correct any errors on the invoice.

earn

to get money in return for labour or services.

earned income

income received for work done, as opposed to unearned income such as rent and interest.

earnings per share

the amount of company earnings available per ordinary share issued. The earnings may be distributed as dividends or used to expand the business. See **dividend (dividend per share)**, **share**.

EBIT

acronym for *earnings before interest and tax* are deducted. Also known as operating earnings.

EC

See **European Community**

e-commerce (ecommerce)

short form for *electronic commerce.* Also written as ecommerce. The buying and selling of goods and services over the Internet and mobile devices. E-commerce uses technologies such as electronic funds transfer, Internet marketing and online transaction systems and inventory management systems. See **electronic funds transfer**, **Internet**, **Internet marketing**, **online shopping**, **smartphone**.

economic equilibrium

See **equilibrium**.

economic globalisation

[gloh-buh-ly-**zay**-shn]

See **globalisation**.

economic goods

goods or services that are useful to people but scarce in relation to their demand. See **free goods**.

economic growth

an increase in the capacity of an economy to produce goods and services, when comparing time period to another. Economic growth is measured by comparing the change in variables such as national output or gross domestic product. See **gross domestic product**, **Fig. 34** (below), **Fig. 35** (p. 99).

economic life

the time span over which the benefits of using an asset are expected to be received.

economic problem

See basic **economic problem**.

economic resources

See **factors of production**, **resources**.

economic rent

the excess in payment received for a good or service over and above the amount

Figure 34 Annual growth (%) of PNG national output

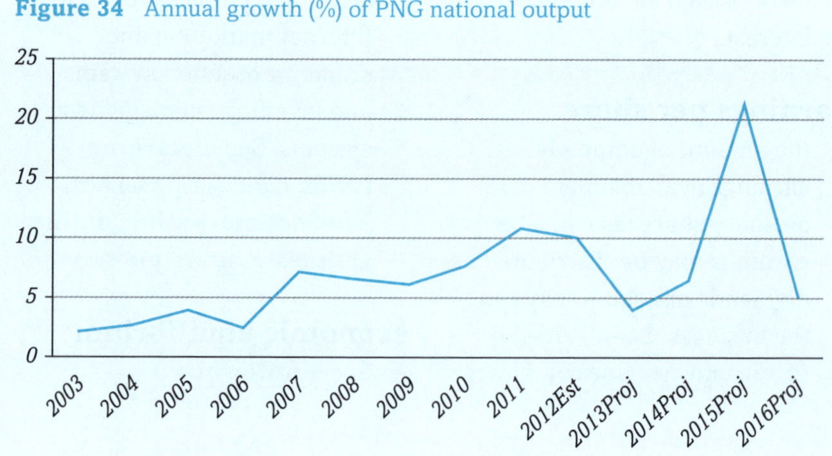

Figure 35 Annual real GDP growth(%) in Japan (1956–2008)

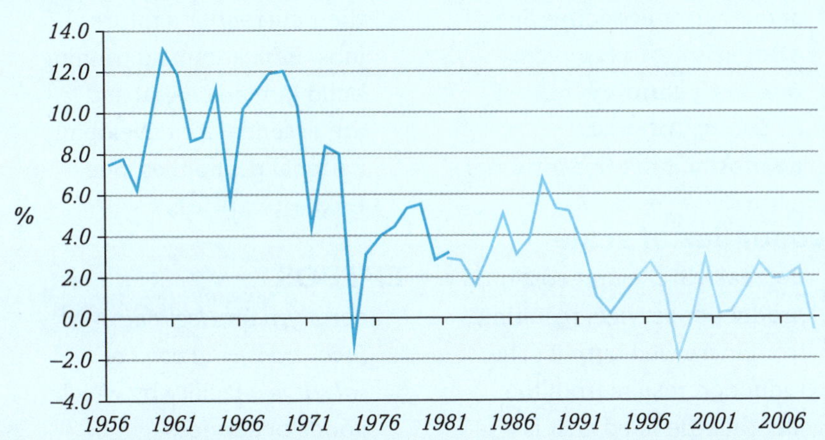

the owner expects. Economic rent arises from conditions of scarcity or strong competition. For example, the owner of an apartment may be willing to rent it out for K2000 per month. But a consumer who likes the location rents the apartment for K3000. The difference of K1000 is the owner's economic rent. See **transfer earnings**.

economics

the study of how individuals, firms, governments and nations make choices in allocating their scarce resources to satisfy their unlimited needs. There are two approaches to economics, the classical and Keynesian approaches. See **allocation of resources**, **classical economics**, **basic economic problem**, **Keynesian economics**, **macroeconomics**, **microeconomics**.

economic system

a system of producing and distributing goods and services and allocating resources in a society. Examples include a market economy, a planned economy, a mixed economy and a barter economy. See **allocation of resources**, **market economy**, **mixed economy**, **planned economy**, **barter economy**.

economies of scale

decrease in the unit cost of a product or service, resulting from increased output. The reduction results from the fact that the fixed cost is being shared over a larger numbers of goods. See **diseconomies of scale**, **fixed cost**.

economist [e-**kon**-o-mist]

an expert in economics.

economy [e-**kon**-o-mi]

everything related to the production and consumption of goods and services in an area. The area could be small or large, a village, a town, a region or a nation.

education and training

all activities that people take part in, to obtain knowledge and learn new skills for their current or a future jobs. Education and training build human capital and are essential for developing national economies. See **human capital**.

EFTPOS

acronym for *electronic funds transfer at point of sale*. It is a facility by which goods or services can be paid for by using a plastic debit card. The card is inserted into an EFTPOS machine at the shop and money is immediately transferred out of the customer's bank account directly into the seller's bank account. The debit card can also be used in an ATM to withdraw cash. See **automatic teller machine (ATM)**, **cash point**, **debit card**, **e-commerce (ecommerce)**, **electronic funds transfer**, **Fig. 36** (p. 101).

Figure 36 EFTPOS card

C smart®

4272 0712 3456 7890

4272

VALID THRU 00/00 *V* Daimlerchrysler Bank

MARIA BARON

elastic

an elasticity greater than 1, which means that the percentage change in one variable is more than the percentage change in another variable. See **elasticity**, **elastic demand**, **elastic supply**.

elastic demand

the situation in which, for a given percentage change in the price of a good or service, there is a greater percentage change in the quantity demanded. Elasticity is greater than 1. See **elastic**, **elasticity**, **elasticity of demand**, **inelastic demand**, **unitary elastic demand**.

elasticity

the effect of a change in one variable on another variable. It is measured as the ratio of the percentage change in one variable to the percentage change of another. **Fig. 37** (p. 102) shows the changes in variable X as variable Y changes between point 1 and point 2 on the curve. It shows that variable X changes in value from X_1 to X_2 in response to variable Y changing from values Y_1 to Y_2.

Figure 37 Elasticity

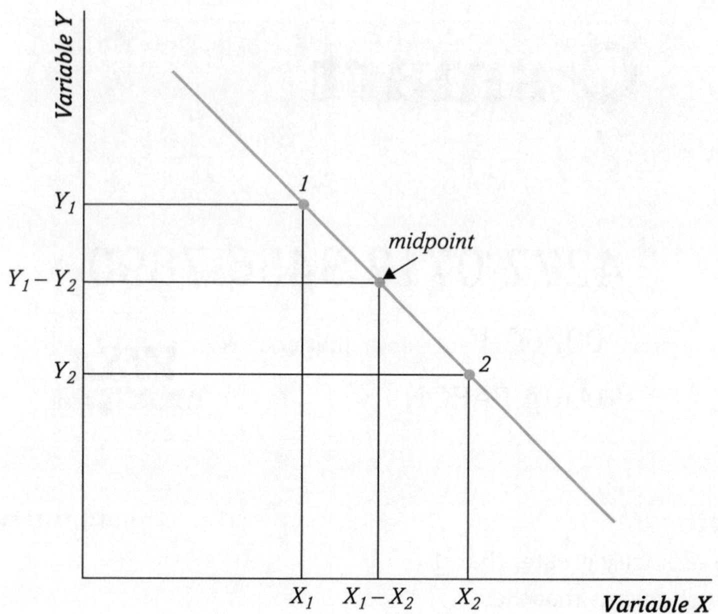

Figure 38 Calculating point elasticity

$$\% \text{ change in X} = \frac{X_2 - X_1}{X_1} \times 100, \text{ where } X_1 = \text{original value of X}$$

$$\% \text{ change in Y} = \frac{Y_2 - Y_1}{Y_1} \times 100, \text{ where } Y_1 = \text{original value of Y}$$

$$E_{x,y} = \frac{X_2 - X_1}{X_1} \times 100 \ / \ \frac{Y_2 - Y_1}{Y_1} \times 100$$

$$= \frac{X_2 - X_1}{Y_2 \ Y_1} \times \frac{Y_1}{X_1}$$

The Y-elasticity of X is defined as:

$$E_{x,y} = \frac{\% \text{ change in variable X}}{\% \text{ change in variable Y}}$$

The negative sign of elasticity is always ignored. Elasticities greater than 1 are called elastic. Those less than1 are

Figure 39 Calculating arc elasticity

$$\% \text{ change in X} = \frac{X_2 - X_1}{(X_2 - X_1)/2} \times 100, \text{ where } (X_2 - X_1)/2 = \text{the mid-point value of X}$$

$$\% \text{ change in Y} = \frac{Y_2 - Y_1}{(Y_2 - Y_1)/2} \times 100, \text{ where } (Y_2 - Y_1)/2 = \text{the mid-point value of Y}$$

$$E_{x,y} = \frac{X_2 - X_1}{(X_2 - X_1)/2} \times 100 / \frac{Y_2 - Y_1}{(Y_2 - Y_1)/2} \times 100$$

$$= \frac{X_2 - X_1}{Y_2 - Y_1} \times \frac{Y_2 - Y_1}{X_2 - X_1}$$

called inelastic. An elasticity of 1 is called unitary.

Elasticity can be measured in two different ways: point elasticity and arc elasticity.

For **point elasticity**, the percentage change in the two variables is calculated relative their original values. See **Fig. 38** (p. 102).

For **arc elasticity,** the change in the two variables is calculated relative to their value mid-point between the original and final values. See **Fig. 39** (above).

See **elastic**, **inelastic**, **unitary elastic**, **Fig. 37** (p. 102), **Fig. 38** (p. 102), **Fig. 39** (above).

elasticity of demand

the ratio of the percentage change in quantity demanded of a good or service to the percentage change in other economic factors such as its price (price elasticity of demand), the price of other goods (cross-elasticity of demand) and consumer income (income elasticity of demand). See **Fig. 40** (p. 104).

elastic supply

the situation in which, for a given percentage change in the price of a good or service, there is a greater percentage change in quantity supplied.

Figure 40 Elasticity of demand

$$\text{Elasticity of demand} = \frac{\%\ \text{change in demand}}{\%\ \text{change in another variable}}$$

Elasticity is greater than 1. See **elastic**, **elasticity**, **elasticity of supply**, **inelastic supply**, **unitary elastic supply**.

elasticity of supply

the ratio of the percentage change in quantity supplied of a good or service to the percentage change of other economic factors such as price (price elasticity of supply) or the price of other goods (cross-elasticity of supply). See **supply**, **elasticity**, **Fig. 41** (below).

electronic commerce (e-commerce or ecommerce)

See **e-commerce (ecommerce)**.

electronic funds transfer

the transfer of money from one account to another account in the same financial institution or in another bank or financial institution, through computer systems. See **EFTPOS**, **electronic commerce**, **Internet marketing**, **online shopping**.

electronic mail

See **email**.

El Niño

originally the name El Niño was given to a warm ocean current that sometimes appears off the coast of Peru (on the west coast of South America). Today EI Niño is used to describe one part of a weather cycle called the El Niño Southern

Figure 41 Elasticity of supply

$$\text{Elasticity of supply} = \frac{\%\ \text{change in supply}}{\%\ \text{change in another variable}}$$

Oscillation (ENSO), which affects the weather in the Pacific and the whole world. At one extreme of the El Niño cycle, the western Pacific experiences high air pressure, cooler oceans, winds from west to east and dry conditions. A severe El Niño event causes droughts and a lack of wet seasons for Indonesia, Papua New Guinea and eastern Australia. Droughts caused by a severe ENSO event drastically affects food security as food production is reduced and water sources that are used to make sago can dry up. At high altitudes, repeated frosts completely disrupt food production because they kill sweet potato plants. Climate change could result in increased frequency and severity of El Niño droughts. See **climate change**, **food security**.

email

a system for sending and receiving messages electronically from one computer to one or more other computers via a computer network or the Internet.

embargo [em-**bahr**-goh]

the banning of trading with a country. The ban can be general, in which case all trading with the country is prohibited, or on specific goods such as weapons.

emigration

See **migration**.

emission [ee-**mi**-shn]

the release of a substance into the atmosphere. When referring to climate change, the substances are usually greenhouse gases. See **greenhouse gas**.

emission allowance

also called emission permits. A permit that allows a company to emit pollutants into the atmosphere. Governments can place a cap or limit on the total amount of pollutants that can be emitted. This limit or cap is then divided up and allocated or sold as emission allowances or permits to companies that emit greenhouse gases and other pollutants. A company must hold enough permits to cover its annual emissions. A company that emits more pollutants than are covered by its allowance must buy allowances or permits from a company that requires fewer emissions or may pay a fine to the regulating authority. See **carbon tax**, **greenhouse gases**, **emission**, **emissions trading**.

emission permit
see **emission allowance**.

emissions trading
also called cap-and-trade. The buying and selling of emission allowances or permits. If a company emits fewer greenhouse gases than permitted by its emission allowance, it can sell the balance of its emissions allowance to another company. The buyer is paying a charge for polluting, while the seller is being rewarded for having reduced its emissions. This creates a cash incentive for companies to reduce their emissions. Thirty-eight countries had emission trading schemes operating at the beginning of 2013. Many other countries, including China, Japan and South Korea, have committed to introducing emissions trading schemes. See **carbon tax**, **greenhouse gas**, **emission**, **emission allowance**.

employee [em-**ploi**-yee]
a person who works for another person or organisation for wages or salary.

employer
a person or organisation that employs people.

employment agency
an organisation that helps people find jobs.

endorse
to sign the back of a cheque or bill of exchange to make it payable to someone other than the payee. See **payee**.

endowment
[en-**daow**-muhnt]
money or property donated to a non-profit organisation or institution in the form of an investment,

with the aim that the dividends will provide a regular income.

endowment policy

an insurance policy (more correctly referred to as a life endowment policy) in which a sum of money is paid after a specific period of time or at death, whichever occurs first.

end-user certificate (EUC)

a document used in international transfers, including sales of weapons and ammunition, to certify that the buyer is the final recipient of the materials, and is not planning to transfer the materials to another party. See **certificate of origin**.

entity

a person, partnership, company, trust or other organisation.

entrepreneur
[ahn-truh-pruh-**nur**]

an individual who, rather than working as an employee, runs a small business, taking on all the risks and enjoying the rewards. Entrepreneurs are commonly seen as business leaders and innovators who turn new ideas into profitable businesses.

entrepreneurship
[ahn-truh-pruh-**nur**-ship]

the skills and willingness to take a new idea and accepting the risks, develop, organise and manage a business venture in order to make a profit. In economics entrepreneurship is classified as one of the four main factors of production. See **factors of production**.

environmental audit
[en-vy-ruhn-**men**-tuhl]

an independent investigation to report on whether an activity complies with environmental legislation and causes the least possible harm to the environment. The audit should also make recommendations on how to reduce any damaging ffects on the environment and how long-term savings could be made by using environmentally friendly technology.

environmental legislation [lej-is-**lay**-shn]
laws, rules and regulations concerned with maintaining and protecting the natural environment. The aim is to limit the amount of pollution and damage to the environment being caused by business and industrial activities. The legislation usually requires companies to undertake environmental audits on existing operations and prepare environmental plans for proposed operations to show what actions will be taken to limit pollution and other environmental damage. See **environmental audit**.

equilibrium [ek-wuh-**lib**-ree-uhm]
a situation in which the supply of a good or service is exactly equal to its demand. Since there is neither surplus nor shortage in the market, price tends to remain stable in this situation. Equilibrium occurs where the supply and demand curves cross and will be automatically reached in a free market. See **changes in equilibrium**, **classical economics**, **equilibrium price**, **Keynesian economics**, **Fig. 19** (p. 51), **Fig. 42** (p. 109).

equilibrium price
the price at which the supply of a good matches demand and where the supply and demand curves cross. It is the price at equilibrium where there is no shortage or surplus. See **changes in equilibrium**, **equilibrium**, **Fig. 19** (p. 51), **Fig. 42** (p. 109).

equilibrium point
See **changes in equilibrium**, **equilibrium**, **equilibrium price**, **Fig. 19** (p. 51), **Fig. 42** (p. 109).

equity [**ek**-wi-tee]
1 a stock or any other security that represents ownership.
2 the value of the funds contributed by shareholders plus the retained earnings or losses (stockholders' equity).

Figure 42 Equilibrium

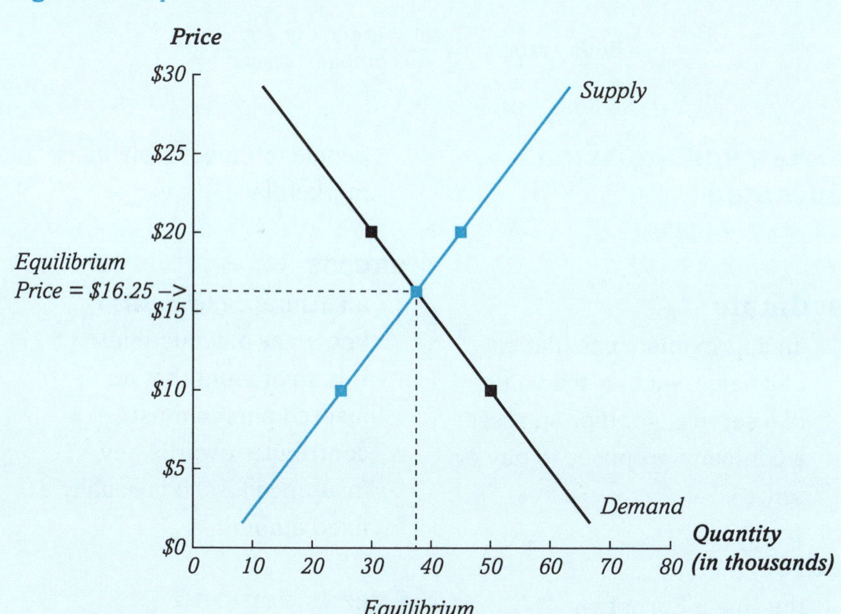

3 the difference between the current value of a property and the amount the owner still owes on a mortgage.

4 the value of a business as measured by the difference between the assets and liabilities of a business.

equity capital

the part of the share capital of a company that is owned by holders of ordinary shares.

equity market

See **stock market**.

equity ratio [**ray**-shee-oh]

ratio of the shareholder equity to the total tangible assets of a company.

The equity ratio measures what proportion of the company's assets has been financed by shareholders rather than through borrowing. See **Fig. 43** (p. 110).

equity share

an ordinary share in a company listed on the stock exchange.

Figure 43 Equity ratio

$$\text{Equity ratio} = \frac{\text{Total shareholder equity}}{\text{Total company assets}}$$

errors and omissions excepted

see **E and OE**.

estimate

an approximate calculation of a value, such as the value of a service, good or an asset a company proposes to buy or sell.

euro

the single European currency, which is now used by 17 member states of the European Union.

European Community

see **European Union**.

European Union (EU)

a group of European countries that participate in the world economy as one economic unit, using one currency: the euro. The EU's goal is to create a barrier-free trade zone to allow money, goods, services and people to move freely in its marketplace.

excess

an insurance term, also known as a deductible. It is an amount that an insured person must contribute towards any insurance loss. It is usually a fixed amount.

excess demand

a situation in which, at a given price, the quantity of a good demanded by consumers in the market is greater than the market supply. Excess demand leads to shortages and causes market prices to rise. See **law of demand**, **demand curve**, **shortage**.

excess supply

a situation in which, at a given price, the quantity of a good supplied in the market is greater than the market demand. Excess supply leads to a surplus and causes market prices to fall. See **law of supply**, **supply curve**, **surplus**.

exchange

1 giving something and receiving something else in return. Barter is a form of exchange.

2 changing some currency of one country to its equivalent in the currency of another country.

3 a marketplace in which securities, commodities, derivatives and other financial instruments are traded. Exchanges ensure fair trading and allow companies, governments and other groups to sell securities to investors.

exchange rate

the value of a currency of one country in relation to the currency of another country. The rate at which one currency can be exchanged for another. See **fixed exchange rate**, **floating exchange rate**, **managed floating exchange rate**, **rate of exchange**.

excise duty

an indirect tax charged on the sale of certain goods produced within a country. All countries in the Pacific region charge an excise tax on tobacco and alcohol. See **customs duty**.

excludable goods

goods that must be paid for in order to be consumed. The consumer can be excluded from consuming the good if they are unwilling to pay for it. Food in a restaurant is excludable. See **non-excludable goods**, **private goods**, **public goods**, **rival goods**.

excludable resource

a good or service that people who have not paid for it can be excluded from using. Examples include food, clothing, cinemas and satellite television.

exclusive economic zone (EEC)

an area of coastal water and seabed within a certain distance of a country's coastline, to which the country claims exclusive rights for fishing, drilling and other economic activities.

exclusion [eks-**kloo**-zhun]
an insurance term which means that some types of losses are not covered by the insurance policy. Examples include damage to property caused by an earthquake or riots.

exclusive dealing
where a retailer or wholesaler is obliged by contract to purchase from the contracted supplier only. See **anti-competitive practices**.

ex dividend
see **dividend**.

executor [egg-**zek**-yoo-ter]
a person or institution appointed by a person making a will to carry out the terms of the will.

ex officio [**eks** uh-**fish**-ee-oh]
Latin for 'from the office', meaning 'by right of office'. See **ex officio member**.

ex officio member
a person who is a member of a board, committee or other official group because of the position she or he holds.

expenditure
money spent on goods and services.

expenses
money spent by a business on goods and services such as rent, wages and insurance.

expertise [eks-per-**teez**]
specialist knowledge or skill possessed by a person or a business.

exporter
a person or company that exports goods or services.

exports
goods and services sent to other countries.

ex ship
the seller pays all costs of shipping of goods to a named port.

external audit
an audit carried out by independent professional accountants. See **audit**, **internal audit**.

external benefits
See **positive externalities**.

external costs of production
when production or consumption of a good imposes costs on a third party. Also called negative externalities. See **externalities**, **negative externalities**.

external economies
See **externalities**.

external economies of scale
the lowering of a firm's costs due to factors outside their control. They are positive externalities that reduce the firm's costs. See **positive externalities**.

externalities
[eks-ter-**nal**-i-teez]
a cost or benefit arising from the production process, which affects people other than the buyer or seller. Also called side effects. External costs or diseconomies of an activity are damages caused to other people or to the environment. For example, pollution of the air or water has in the past not been paid for by those who cause it. Carbon tax is an effort by some governments to make polluters pay for the external costs of their air pollution. External benefits or economies are free, pleasant or profitable effects to other people resulting from the activity. For example, bees kept for honey production fertilise fruit trees of nearby farmers. See **carbon tax**, **negative externalities**, **positive externalities**.

extraordinary general meeting [ek-**straw**-dn-air-ee]
a special meeting of shareholders of a company or members of a club called to discuss some special business.

extraordinary item
in a set of accounts, an item of revenue and expense, and other gains and losses in the period, which are the result of events or transactions outside the ordinary operations. Examples could include gains or losses from the sale of investments, or losses caused by fire, earthquakes, cyclones, and floods. See **abnormal item**.

face value

the value printed on a coin, banknote or financial document.

facsimile machine

[fak-**sim**-uh-lee]

an electronic machine, also called a fax machine, that uses standard telephone lines to transmit and receive text and images. Email and the Internet now provide a much cheaper method of transmitting text and images. But many businesses still maintain a fax machine because in some countries contracts transmitted by email and the Internet are not recognised by law, while signed faxed contracts are.

factoring

1 buying goods for resale without further processing.

2 buying debts due from another firm's customers, usually at a discount, and collecting them.

factor inputs

See **factors of production**.

factor rewards

payments made to the owners of resources or factors of production. Owners of natural resources receive rent and royalties, providers of labour receive wages, investors receive interest on capital and entrepreneurs receive profit. See **factors of production**.

factors of production

the inputs used in the production of goods and services. The main factors of production are:

- land, which includes natural resources. See **land**.
- labour provided by workers. See **labour**.
- capital. See **capital.**
- the entrepreneurship of individuals who accept the risks and develop, organise and manage a business venture in order to make a profit. See **entrepreneurship**.

factory

a building or group of buildings where goods are manufactured or assembled.

factory overheads

also called manufacturing overheads. The total cost of operating a factory. It includes such expenses as insurance, depreciation, maintenance and repair of the factory building, and machinery and power used in the factory.

failed state

a general term describing a country that has no control over its territory, cannot provide peace and security for its people, and cannot or does not provide public services.

fair trade

agreements that make sure that farmers, particularly those in developing countries, are paid a fair price for their produce. Produce purchased under these agreements is certified and stamped as 'fair trade' products.

FAS

acronym for *free alongside ship*. It means that the price paid includes the delivery of the goods to a port where it will be placed within reach of a ship's lifting cranes and tackle. Any further costs, such as loading, insurance and freight charges, must be paid for by the buyer.

fast food

easily prepared food sold in a snack bar or restaurant, usually as a quick, take-away meal.

fax

see **facsimile machine**.

feasibility study

[fee-zuh-**bil**-i-tee]

an analysis of whether a proposed project can be completed successfully. The study should advise managers of the possible negative and positive outcomes of a project, helping them decide whether they should proceed.

fee

an amount paid for a professional service.

feedback

part of a two-way process by which customers provide information about their reaction to a product or service, which producers can use to make changes or improvements.

fiduciary

[fi-**dyoo**-shee-air-ee]

a person legally appointed and authorised to hold and manage assets in trust for another person.

FIFO

See **first in, first out**.

file

a place where documents and letters are kept in a logical order, for easy reference.

final accounts

usually refers to the profit and loss account and balance sheet.

final demand

the last request for payment of a debt before court action is taken to recover the debt.

final dividend

see **dividend**.

final good

see **consumer good**.

finance

1 providing money, usually in the form of a loan for a person or a business.

2 the management of money, banking, investment and credit for a government or a large company. For example the Department of Finance.

finance house

a business that lends money against collateral to other businesses and individuals, especially in the financing of hire-purchase contracts. The interest charged is usually higher than that charged by banks. Also called a finance company.

financial account

See **capital account**.

financial accountant

an accountant who is mainly responsible for the preparation of the profit and loss account and balance sheet, monthly and annually.

financial adviser
a person or business that helps individuals or businesses manage their finances by providing investment advice.

financial intermediaries [in-tuh-**mee**-dee-air-eez]
institutions, such as a banks, building societies or provident and pension funds, that hold funds from lenders and savers and make loans to borrowers.

financial statement
records that outline the financial activities of a business, organisation or individual. For businesses, financial statements usually include the balance sheet, income statement, statement of retained earnings and cash flows.

financial year
the period used by businesses for calculating annual ('yearly') financial statements. The dates differ in various countries. In Papua New Guinea the financial year is 1 January – 31 December, the same as the calendar year. In Australia, the financial year starts on 1 July and ends on 30 June the next year. See **fiscal year**.

firm
another term for a business organisation. See **company**, **corporation**, **partnership**, **sole proprietor**.

first in, first out (FIFO)
a method of accounting used for stock sold in order of time. When charging stock to the cost, it is assumed that when the business uses materials or sells goods, those that have been held in stock the longest are used or sold first.

fiscal policy [**fis**-kuhl]
how a government changes its tax rates and spending to influence the nation's economy. For example, if consumer spending needs to be reduced in order to control inflation, governments can increase income tax, which reduces consumers' disposable income, leaving them with

less money to spend. See **Keynesian economics**.

fiscal year
the government's financial year. In Papua New Guinea the fiscal year is the same as the financial year. In the US the fiscal year starts on 1 October and ends on 30 September the following year. See **financial year**.

fixed asset
assets such as buildings and machinery that are bought for long-term use. Also called non-current assets. Each year, a proportion of the purchase price of a fixed asset is generally written off against profits as depreciation. See **non-current assets**, **depreciation**, **write off**.

fixed-assets register
a record in a business of all the fixed assets owned by the business. See **fixed asset**.

fixed capital
assets or capital needed to start a business and not used up in the actual production of a good or service. They include anything that is not continually purchased for the production process. Examples include factories, office buildings, computer servers, insurance policies, legal contracts and manufacturing equipment. See **fixed asset**.

fixed costs
those costs that must be incurred in fixed quantity, regardless of the level of output produced. Examples include rent, depreciation and insurance. See **average fixed cost**, **Fig. 25** (p. 71).

fixed exchange rate
a system in which a currency's exchange rate is maintained at a fairly constant rate against one, or a basket of, strong currencies. The country needs to have large foreign exchange reserves to be able to fix its exchange rate. See **basket**, **floating exchange rate**, **foreign exchange reserves**, **managed exchange rate**.

Figure 44 Calculation of rate interest

Loan of K1000 at 10% interest payable over 3 years	
Interest each year = 10% of K1000	= K100
Total interest over 3 years = 3 × K100	= K300
Total amount to be repaid = principal + interest	
	= K1000 + K300
	= K1300

fixed expenses

expenses that do not change from one accounting period to another, such as loan repayments and rent.

fixed-term liability

the heading under which a fixed-term loan is shown in a balance sheet. It is a liability repayable on a particular date in the future. See **fixed-term loan**.

fixed-term loan

a loan that must be repaid by a certain date. See **fixed-term liability**.

flat rate of interest

a fixed amount of interest charged on the full amount of the original loan. It does not reduce as the loan is gradually being repaid. The true rate of interest is thus much higher than the flat rate of interest (approximately twice as high). See **Fig. 44** (above).

flexible budget

[**flek**-suh-bul]

a business budget showing the estimated net profit at different levels of output or sales. See **budget**.

flexitime

a system of working a set number of hours each week, with the starting and finishing time each day set by the employee.

float [floht]

see **cash float**.

floating charge
a security similar to a mortgage. A company can obtain a loan from a bank, which uses the company's assets as a floating charge to secure the loan. The amount borrowed can change depending on the value of the company's assets. The company can continue to operate, although the bank can liquidate the company and sell off its assets if the company fails to make repayments by the due date. See **mortgage.**

floating exchange rate
where the exchange rate for a country's currency is determined by the foreign exchange market. See **exchange rate**, **fixed exchange rate**, **foreign exchange market**, **managed exchange rate**.

floating rate of exchange
See **floating exchange rate**.

floating rate of interest
an interest rate on a loan such as a mortgage, which moves up or down in line with market rates. See **fixed interest rate**.

float of shares
See **flotation**.

floor price
the lowest price for a commodity that a controlling group will allow. For example, a government authority such as a copra marketing board can set a lowest acceptable price for copra. If market prices begin to fall, it can try to stop the market price falling below the floor price (either by buying all the offered copra at that price, or by restricting the supply of copra to the market until prices rise).

flotation [floh-**tay**-shn]
the process of issuing shares in a newly established or existing private company, for public sale to investors. The company 'goes private' and its shares are listed on the stock exchange. The process is also used for the privatisation of state-owned enterprises.

flow chart

a business chart showing the steps that are taken in a business activity.

FOB

acronym for *free on board.* The selling price includes the cost of loading the goods onto the ship. The buyer is then responsible for all other charges, including freight and insurance. See **acronym**, **CAF**, **CIF**.

food security

access by all people at all times to sufficient, affordable, nutritious, culturally appropriate food so as to allow them to lead healthy and productive lives. Food security for the majority of rural people in the Pacific region is provided for by subsistence agriculture. Climate change and global warming along with HIV/AIDS and the threat of El Niño droughts are the main threats to food security for rural people. See **AIDS**, **climate change**, **El Niño**, **HIV**.

footnotes

data provided in addition to a financial statement. Footnotes should explain financial statement figures and any other matters necessary to help give a clear picture of a company's financial position. See **financial statement**.

forecasting [**fohr**-kast-ing]

the process of making predictions about future economic and market conditions. Information used in forecasting includes data from the past, surveys on what business people expect to happen, and proposed government policy.

foreclosure [fohr-**kloh**-zher]

the taking over of a mortgaged property by the lender because the borrower has failed to make repayments by the due date.

foreign aid

grants, concessional loans and technical assistance provided to promote economic development and welfare. It is provided by the government of a foreign country or by a multi-nation agency such as the World Bank. Foreign aid is not always free, because it may come with economic and political conditions. In many cases, donors require that the receiving country undertake reforms that the donors believe will promote economic growth or development. See **concessional loan**, **tied aid**, **untied aid**.

foreign currency

the currency of another country. See **foreign currency account**, **foreign currency exchange**.

foreign currency account

an account in a bank in a currency of another country. For example, a bank account in US dollars held in a bank in Papua New Guinea.

foreign exchange

1 the exchange of one currency for another, or the conversion of one currency into another currency.

2 the global market where currencies are traded virtually around the clock. See **foreign exchange market**.

usually abbreviated as 'forex' or occasionally as 'FX'.

foreign exchange control

a system under which any holder of national currency requires official approval from the central bank to convert it into a foreign currency. See **capital controls**.

foreign exchange market

the market in which foreign currencies are bought and sold. There is no one place for this market, with trading taking place via computers and telephone connections. The total value of foreign exchange trading worldwide is many times more than the value of the total international trade in goods and services. See **foreign currency**.

foreign exchange reserves

assets held by a country's government or central bank, such as gold, and cash and securities in hard currencies such as US dollars or euro. A government can use its foreign exchange reserves to support the value of its own currency in the foreign exchange market. See **hard currency**, **fixed exchange rate**, **managed exchange rate**, **managed floating exchange rate**.

foreign investment
the purchase by residents of a country of assets overseas is called outward foreign investment. The investment by foreign nationals in assets in the country is called inward foreign investment.

foreman
a person who supervises a group of production workers. Now usually called a foreperson.

forex
the abbreviation for *foreign exchange*.

forge [fawj]
to copy a signature, letter or other document and pretend that it is genuine, usually for an illegal purpose. See **forgery**.

forgery [**fohr**-juh-ree]
an illegal copy of a banknote, a document or a signature.

forward contract
See **futures contract**.

forward integration
See **vertical integration**.

fossil fuel
fuel such as coal, oil or natural gas, formed from the carbon remains of once-living plants and animals. See **non-renewable resources**.

4G
the fourth generation of a mobile broadband communication system, which is replacing 3G. Users in the few countries that have 4G networks report being able to download information from the Internet up to 10 times faster than with 3G. See **3G**.

franchise [**fran**-chyz]
a licence that one well-known business (franchisor) gives to

another business (franchisee) to sell a product or provide a service under the franchisor's business name. In exchange, the franchisee pays the franchisor an initial fee and an annual licence fee. Hilton Hotels and McDonalds are examples of franchises.

franked dividends
dividends paid by companies on which tax has already been paid. See **dividend**.

fraud [frawd]
obtaining money, goods or services illegally by deceiving someone.

free alongside ship
See **FAS**.

free enterprise
an economy in which the majority of economic activities are organised through the free market. See **centrally planed economy**, **free market**, **laissez-faire**.

free goods
goods, such as air and water, which are abundant and not considered scarce. Because such goods have no opportunity costs they are often used in large quantities and their overuse often causes pollution. See **economic goods**.

freehold
permanent ownership of land, including the right to sell it.

freelance
a self-employed person who works on assignments for a number of different of clients.

free market
a market in which people buy and sell goods without outside control on the quantity or price of goods traded. See **free enterprise**, **free-market economy**, **laissez-faire**.

free-market economy
an economy in which the majority of economic activities are organised through the free market. See **centrally planed economy**, **free enterprise**, **free market**, **laissez-faire**.

free on board
See **FOB**.

free rider
someone who enjoys the benefits of public goods or services without having to contribute to their cost.

free trade
a policy of international trade without barriers such as tariffs, subsidies, quotas or other trade restrictions.

free trade agreement
an agreement between two or more countries to set up a free trade area. See **free trade area**.

free trade area
a group of countries with free trade between them. See **free trade**.

free trade zone
a area within a country, usually around an airport or port, into which goods are allowed to be imported free of customs duties or other tariffs as long as they are exported or used to produce goods that are exported. Import duties are, however, charged on goods that are distributed to other parts of the country outside the free trade zone.

freight
cost of transporting goods.

frictional unemployment [**frik**-shn-ul]
unemployment that is always present in the economy and is caused by people in the process of moving from one job to another or from one location to another. See **cyclical unemployment**, **structural unemployment**.

fringe benefits [frinj]
goods or services given to an employee in addition to a wage or salary. Examples of fringe benefits include a company car or a car allowance, private health insurance or a housing allowance. See **perks**, **net advantages of a job**.

fuel
a substance that burns to produce energy. Fuels are humans' main source of energy, without which very few economic activities are

possible. The fossil fuels such as natural gas, oil and coal are the main forms of energy used to produce electricity for production. These fuels are also the greatest contributors to greenhouse gases, air pollution and global warming. See **alternative energy**, **fossil fuels**, **greenhouse gases**, **air pollution**, **renewable energy**.

full employment

a situation in which every worker available for employment has a job. It is unlikely that this can ever be achieved, even if there were excess demand in the labour market. There will always be some level of unemployment. For example, there will always be people moving from one job to another, people with unrealistic expectations and those whose past conduct make sit hard for them to find employment. See **frictional unemployment**.

functions of money

the roles played by money in an economy, which include a medium for exchange for goods and services, a standard of value, and a store of value and wealth. See **bitcoin**, **exchange rate**, **medium of exchange**, **money**, **store of value**.

fundamentals

[fuhn-duh-**men**-tlz]

information that can give an indication of value and growth potential. The balance sheet, the income statement, management and cash flow are the fundamentals of a company. A company with little debt and a lot of cash is said to have strong fundamentals.

funding

1 the act of providing money to finance a particular purpose, program or project.
2 the money provided to finance a particular purpose, program or project.

futures

See **futures contract**.

futures contract

a contract to buy or sell a good, share or currency by a certain date at an agreed price.

Futures can be used to reduce risk or to speculate on the price movement of an asset. For example, a producer of gold could use futures to lock in a certain price on a set date and protect themselves against loss if the price falls. On the other hand, anybody could speculate (gamble) on the price movement of gold by going long or short using futures contracts. See **commodities futures**, **futures market**, **long**, **short**, **options contract**.

futures market

a market in which futures contracts are bought and sold.

gain

an increase in profit or wealth.

garnishee order

[gahr-ni-**shee**]

a court order requiring money to be taken from a debtor's wages and paid directly to a creditor.

GATT

see **General Agreement on Tariffs and Trade**.

GDP

see **gross domestic product**.

gearing

the level of a company's debt, usually measured as a percentage of the ration of debt to shareholder equity. High gearing refers to high debt and low gearing refers to low debt. See **leverage**, **Fig. 45** (below).

General Agreement on Tariffs and Trade (GATT)

an agreement drawn up in 1947 to reduce trade barriers by the elimination of tariffs and other forms of import control. GATT was absorbed into the World Trade Organization (WTO) in 1994. See **barriers to trade**, **Doha Round**, **tariff**, **World Trade Organization (WTO)**, **Uruguay Round**.

general average

in insurance terms, a reference to cargo being thrown

Figure 45 Gearing

$$\text{Gearing (\%)} = \frac{\text{Debts (shot- and long-term debt + overdrafts etc.)}}{\text{shareholder equity}} \times 100\%$$

overboard to save a ship from sinking. The owners of the ship and cargo saved by this action share responsibility for the loss.

gift

a legal term describing the giving of a valuable item such as money, property or shares during a person's lifetime, rather than leaving them to someone in a will.

gift voucher

a card or letter that can be exchanged for goods up to a stated value at a certain store or stores. Gift vouchers are normally purchased and given to someone as a present. They are sometimes given away as prizes in competitions.

gilt-edged security

high-grade investment with very low risk. They include bonds issued by governments or the stocks or bonds issued by well-established, financially stable companies that can be relied on to pay the dividends or interest.

global economics

See **globalisation**.

globalisation

[gloh-buh-ly-**zay**-shn]

the ongoing process by which the world is moving towards a single market with goods, services, capital and labour being traded on a worldwide basis.

global warming

a rise in the average temperature of the Earth and its atmosphere. Scientists believe that this is being caused in part by the increase of greenhouse gases in the atmosphere resulting from the emissions of fossil fuel-burning power stations and factories. Global warming is responsible for climate change, the melting of polar ice sheets and glaciers and a rise in sea levels. See **climate change**, **emissions**, **greenhouse effect**, **greenhouse gas**, **sea-level rise**.

GNI

See **gross national income**.

GNP

See **gross national product**.

going concern

a business which is regarded as financially stable and likely to be able to continue trading in the future.

goods

tangible outputs that can be seen, stored, transported and sold.

goodwill

the reputation and good name of a business that is considered a valuable asset. A value for goodwill is therefore included as part of the price when the business is sold.

government expenditure

All money spent by government on goods, services and the servicing of debts.

government intervention

when government takes action to control or change a free market for economic, social or political reasons. See **allocation of resources**, **centrally planned economy**, **free-market economy**, **Keynesian economics**.

government sector

government departments that collect taxes, redistribute income through benefits and subsidies, control and administer the economy and provide public goods such as roads, schools and hospitals. See **circular flow**, **public sector**, **Fig. 22** (p. 54).

government stock

a bond issued against a loan to the government by individuals or companies.

graph

a diagram showing the relationship between two variable quantities. A sales graph shows changes in sales against time. See **Fig. 46** (p. 131).

gratis [**grah**-tis]

Latin word meaning free or without payment.

gratuity [gruh-**tyoo**-i-tee]

money paid to an employee at the end of agreed periods, such as yearly, or on retirement.

Figure 46 Sales graph

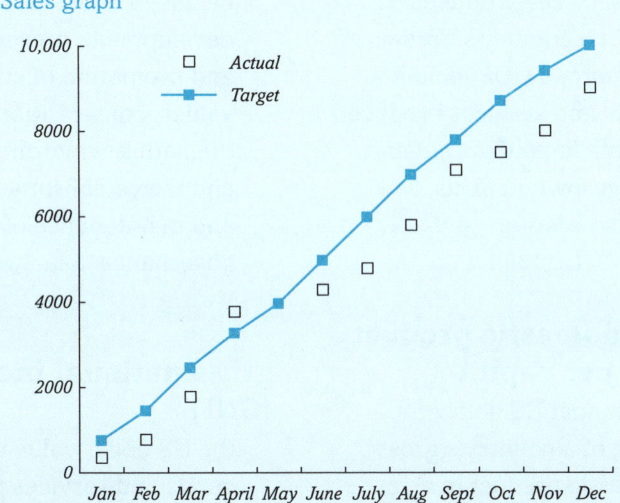

greenhouse effect

the trapping of thermal energy (heat) by the greenhouse gases in the Earth's atmosphere. The gases act like a blanket around the planet, trapping heat and contributing to global warming and climate change. See **climate change**, **greenhouse gas**, **global warming**.

greenhouse gas

any gas in the atmosphere that absorbs and reflects back thermal energy (heat) radiated from the Earth. Carbon dioxide and methane are the most important greenhouse gases. See **climate change**, **emissions**, **fossil fuel**, **global warming**, **greenhouse effect**.

gross

an amount without any deductions. Examples include gross pay before deduction of tax, and gross profit before deductions for overhead, payroll, taxation and interest payments. See **net**, **net income**, **net profit**.

gross domestic product (GDP)

the annual US dollar value of the total output of goods

and services produced within a country's borders. A country's GDP includes goods and services produced by both locally owned and foreign-owned firms. See **gross national income**, **Fig. 47** (p. 133).

gross domestic product (GDP) per capita

the annual US dollar value of a country's gross domestic product in a year, divided by its population in the same year. See **gross domestic product**, **Fig. 47** (p. 133).

gross income

an amount of income before the deduction of taxation.

gross national happiness (GNH)

an index developed in the Himalayan country of Bhutan to measure quality of life not only in economic but also in social and spiritual terms. The index reflects Bhutan's national philosophy that while growth is important, it should be balanced with sustainable development, preservation and promotion of cultural values, conservation of the natural environment, and the establishment and maintenance of good governance. See **standard of living**.

gross national income (GNI)

the US dollar value of all goods and services produced by nationally owned firms and citizens, both within the country and overseas. Income and profits earned by foreigners and foreign-owned companies that are transferred out of a country do not count towards the country's GNI.

The GNI of most Pacific countries is less than their GDP. This is because the value of earnings of citizens transferred into the country from overseas is less than the earnings of foreigners and foreign-owned firms being transferred out of the country. See **gross domestic product**, **Fig. 47** (p. 133).

Figure 47 2012 GDP per capita and GNI per capita

Country	*GDP per capita (US$)**	*GNI per capita (US$)#*	*% Difference*
Australia	41 954	59 570	42%
New Zealand	29 500	24 805	−16%
New Caledonia	37 700	15 000	−60%
East Timor	20 113	3 670	−82%
Tonga	7 987	4 240	−47%
Kiribati	6 241	2 260	−64%
Samoa	6 157	3 320	−46%
Indonesia	4 923	3 420	−31%
Vanuatu	4 843	3 080	−36%
Fiji	4 740	4 200	−11%
Solomon Islands	3 288	1 130	−66%
Papua New Guinea	2 736	1 790	−35%

gross national income (GNI) per capita

the US dollar value of a country's gross national income in a year, divided by its population of the same year. It reflects the average income of a country's citizens. See **gross national income**, **Fig. 47** (above).

gross national product (GNP)

See **gross national income**.

gross profit

the difference between the sale price and the cost of the manufacturing or purchasing goods, before deductions for overheads, payroll, taxation and interest payments. See **net profit**.

growth

See **economic growth**.

guarantee [gar-uhn-**tee**]

1 an undertaking by one person to meet the financial debt of another person if the latter fails to pay the debt;

2 an undertaking given by a producer taking responsibility for the quality or performance of goods and services and, if necessary, to repair or replace them.

haggle

a type of negotiation in which a buyer will try to get the price down. If the buyer and seller can agree on a price, a sale will take place. Otherwise no sale will be made. See **bargaining**.

handbook

a book giving useful information about a particular subject or instructions on how to operate a machine.

handle

to manage and have responsibility, such as a shipping agent handling the delivery of goods.

handout

1 a sheet of printed information given out at a conference, seminar, training session or meeting.

2 an amount of goods or money given to people in need, such as victims of floods or cyclones.

hard copy

a printed version of data and information stored in a computer. See **soft copy**.

hard currency

a foreign currency that is in high demand in the foreign exchange market. Hard currencies are usually those of countries that have a strong economy and whose value is expected to remain stable or rise. Hard currencies are the preferred currencies of a country's foreign exchange reserve. See **foreign exchange reserve**.

hard disk

a magnetic disk sealed in a box called a disk drive, hard drive or hard disk drive, on which information is stored.

hard disk drive

See **hard disk**.

head office

the headquarters of an organisation that controls and takes full responsibility for the operations of the organisation.

hedging [**hej**-ing]

activities designed to remove some of the risk in other financial activities. For example, a business such as a gold mine risks making a loss if the price of gold falls. It can reduce that risk by selling a futures contract or call that gives it the option to sell the gold at a fixed price on some date in the future.

Another company, such as a flour mill that needs to buy wheat, faces the risk of the price of wheat rising. It can reduce this risk by buying a futures contract or call that gives it the option to buy the wheat at a fixed price on some date in the future. See **call**, **futures contract**, **options contract**, **put**.

hedge fund [hej]

managed portfolio of investments that uses advanced investment strategies such as leveraged, long, short and derivative positions in both domestic and international markets with the goal of generating high returns. Similar to mutual funds in that investments are pooled and professionally managed, but differ in that membership requires large financial resources. Hedge funds have been called 'mutual funds for the super-rich'. See **derivative**, **leverage**, **long**, **short**.

hidden unemployment

a situation in which people are technically employed, but have zero or very low productivity. This happens where governments employ large numbers of people. See **disguised unemployment**.

highly geared

see **gearing**.

hire

the use by an individual or business of an asset that is leased for a short time. Hiring allows a business to have use of an asset for a short time without the expense of purchasing.

hire purchase (HP)

a system in which good are made available for immediate use but payment is made in instalments. The cost of goods bought on HP is greater than the price for a cash payment, because interest is charged on the outstanding amount. The seller can reclaim the goods if payments are not made on time.

historical cost

in accounting, where the value of an asset on the balance sheet is based on its original cost less depreciation. See **carrying value**, **depreciation**.

historical-cost accounting

accounting for transactions in a business by recording everything at its cost price, even if its value has changed significantly. Depreciation based on the actual cost is deducted from fixed (or non-current) assets each year, so that the value of a fixed asset is shown at its carrying value. See **carrying value**, **depreciation**.

HIV

the abbreviation for 'human immunodeficiency virus', the virus that causes AIDS. HIV is passed from human to human by contact with an infected person's blood, saliva or semen. It is most commonly spread by unprotected sexual relations between men and women, or men and men, or by sharing the same needle for injecting drugs. HIV cannot be caught by touching or even kissing an infected person, or drinking and eating from the same plates and cups. See **AIDS**, **HIV positive**.

HIV/AIDS

See **HIV positive**.

HIV positive

having antibodies against the HIV virus (the antigen) in the blood. This means that the person has already been infected by the HIV virus and is said to have HIV/AIDS. An infected person can pass on the virus to another person. See **AIDS**, **antiretroviral drug**, **HIV**.

holder in due course

usually refers to a person who has the rightful possession of a cheque.

holding company

a company whose only function is holding shares in other companies. The other companies are called subsidiary companies.

holiday pay

payment to an employee during a period of entitled holidays.

homogeneous product

[hoh-muh-**jee**-nee-uhs]

products that are in competition with each other, but between which there is little or no difference.

honour

to pay a cheque or bill of exchange when it is due.

horizontal integration

the amalgamation or joining together of firms who produce the same type of goods or services. For example, the joining together of two mining companies or two banks.

hot money

short-term investments by investors who move their money from one country to another in search of the best interest rates.

hourly rate

the amount paid for each hour worked by an employee.

household

a group of consumers, usually a family or extended family, who live in the same house.

human capital

the total skills, knowledge, attitudes and cultural assets of individuals. Human capital can be used to create economic value for individuals, a company or a country.

human development index (HDI)

a tool developed by the United Nations, which combines life expectancy, education and income in order to rate, rank and classify a country's level of social and economic development. See **Fig. 48** (p. 138).

Figure 48 Human development indices (2013)

Country	*HDI*	*Rank*	*Category*
Australia	0.938	2	Very high
Fiji	0.702	96	Medium
Indonesia	0.629	121	Medium
Japan	0.912	10	Very high
Kiribati	0.629	121	Medium
New Zealand	0.919	6	Very high
Papua New Guinea	0.466	156	Low
Solomon Islands	0.530	143	Low
Timor-Leste	0.576	134	Medium
Vanuatu	0.626	124	Medium

human resource management

the management of an organisation's workforce. It is responsible for the selection, training and performance evaluation of employees.

human resources

the quantity and quality of human effort that goes into the production of goods and services. See **human capital**, **labour**.

hyperinflation

[hy-per-in-**flay**-shn]

extremely rapid inflation. In the mid-1990s, Brazil experienced a rise in prices of about 300% in one year. In Bolivia in the 1980s the inflation rate was 20 000% in one year. Prices rise so quickly during hyperinflation that money almost loses its value as a commodity. See **deflation**, **inflation**, **stagflation**.

illegal
not allowed by law.

illegal activity
any activity that is prohibited by law and therefore not included in a country's national income accounts. Drug smuggling, for example, is an illegal activity and cannot be included as part of a country's legal economic activities. See **black market**.

illegal contract
a contract that is not legal and is not enforceable at law.

ILO
see **International Labour Organization**.

IMF
see **International Monetary Fund**.

immigration
See **migration**.

imperfect competition
a situation in which a large producer or consumer has control over the price of a good or service.

imported inflation
inflation due to an increase in the price of imported goods. For example, increases in the prices of imported fuel and materials increase the costs of local production and therefore the selling prices of locally produced goods.

imports
goods or services produced overseas and brought into a country for local consumption.

import control
government control of the amount and type of goods brought into a country.

import duty
a tax on goods brought into a country.

import licence

a document issued by a government, allowing certain goods to be brought into a country.

import quota

a limit placed by a government on the quantity of a good that can be brought into the country. Quotas are often imposed to protect domestic production. See **import control**, **protectionism**.

import substitution

the strategy by a developing country to replace imported goods with locally produced substitutes. See **substitute good**.

importer

an individual or business that imports goods from a foreign country.

impulse buying

the buying of a good or service without having planned to do so.

incentive

a thing that motivates or encourages someone to do something. Examples include:

- the provision of grants to farmers to improve land.
- the offering of tax exemptions to investors for investing in a new industry or a depressed area. See **tax free holiday**, **tax incentive**.
- bonuses or extra payments for workers exceeding production or sales targets. See **bonus**.

income

1 salary or wages received for work done.

2 rent, interest, dividends or profit received from an investment.

income and expenditure account

the annual account prepared by clubs, societies and other non-profit organisations, showing the financial results for the year. The equivalent of the profit and loss account produced by a business.

income elasticity of demand

a measure of the effect of a change in consumer income on demand. Income elasticity of demand is calculated as

Figure 49 Income elasticity of demand

$$\text{Income elasticity of demand} = \frac{\%\ \text{change in quantity demanded}}{\%\ \text{change in income}}$$

the ratio of the percentage change in demand for a good or service to the percentage change in consumer income. See **demand elasticity**, **elasticity**, **inferior good**, **luxuries**, **price elasticity of demand**, **Fig. 49** (above).

income tax

a direct tax levied by government on earnings.

incorporated land groups (ILGs)

See **land groups**, **land registration**.

increment [**in**-kruh-ment]

an increase in salary.

increasing returns to scale

See **economies of scale**, **returns to scale**.

indemnity [in-**dem**-ni-tee]

1 an insurance term meaning compensation for loss suffered.

2 legal protection against liability for loss or damages. An example is the indemnity given to directors of companies to protect them from being personally liable for company losses due to bad decisions.

indent [**in**-dent]

an official order for goods.

indenture [in-**den**-cher]

a legal written agreement or contract.

indexation [in-dek-**say**-shn]

the automatic adjustment of wages or a value, such as that of the value of property for insurance purposes in proportion to changes in a price index such as the CPI. See **base year**, **consumer price index (CPI)**, **index linked**, **Fig. 24** (p. 67).

index-linked

having a value determined in proportion to changes in

a price index such as the CPI. Pensions, for example, are often index-linked to the CPI. See **base year**, **consumer price index (CPI)**, **indexation**, **Fig. 24** (p. 67).

indirect cost
a cost that is not actually related to the production of a good or service. These include such items as rent, light, power. administrative expenses and depreciation.

indirect tax
a tax on goods or services collected by a third party (such as a retailer) who then passes it on to the government. For example, a value added tax (VAT).

industrial action
action taken by a group of workers, such as a stop work, or strike, over working conditions or pay or both.

industrial dispute
a disagreement between employees and employers about pay or working conditions, or both. If unsolved, such a dispute can lead to industrial action. See **industrial action**.

industrial relations
the relationship between management and workers.

industrial union
See **union**.

industrialisation
[in-duhs-tree-uh-ly-**zay**-shn]
the development of a country's manufacturing sector. The process of expanding the country's capacity to produce secondary goods and services.

industry
a group of related economic activities producing similar goods or services. Examples include the manufacturing industry, construction industry and tourism industry.

inefficiency
not making the best use of labour, time and capital when providing a service or producing something.

inefficient
1 not having the skills or ability to work effectively.

2 not producing the required results.

inelastic

an elasticity of less than 1, which means that the percentage change in one variable is less than the percentage change in another variable. See **elastic**, **elasticity**, **inelastic demand**, **inelastic supply**, **unitary elasticity**.

inelastic demand

the situation in which the percentage change in demand for a good or service is less than the percentage change in its price. Elasticity is less than 1. See **demand elasticity**, **elasticity**, **elastic**, **unitary elastic demand**.

inelastic supply

the situation in which the percentage change in supply of a good or service is less than the percentage change in its price. Elasticity is less than 1. See **supply elasticity**, **elasticity**, **elastic**, **unitary elastic supply**.

infant industries

a newly established industry developed by private enterprise or government. Infant industries are often part of the industrialisation programs of developing countries.

infant mortality rate

[mawr-**tal**-i-tee]

the ratio of the number of deaths of babies under one year old to the number of live births in the same period of time.

inferior good

good whose demand decreases as consumer incomes increase. Has a negative elasticity of demand. These are usually low-quality, cheap versions of a product. See **income elasticity of demand**.

inflation [in-**flay**-shn]

the continual and steady increase in prices of goods and services. Inflation is measured as the percentage increase in the consumer price index (CPI). As inflation rises, there is a fall in the purchasing power of money. See **consumer price index (CPI)**,

Figure 50 Inflation rate calculation

CPI as of end of 1st quarter 2013	= 130
CPI as of end of 2nd quarter 2013	= 132
Increase in CPI in 2nd quarter 2013	= 2
Inflation rate for 2nd quarter 2013 = % rise of CPI = 2/130	= 1.53%

Figure 51 Annual inflation as measured by the increase in consumer price index (CPI)

Country	*2009*	*2010*	*2011*	*2012*
Australia	1.8%	2.8%	3.4%	1.8%
Fiji	3.7%	5.5%	8.7%	3.4%
Indonesia	4.8%	5.1%	5.4%	4.3%
New Zealand	2.1%	2.3%	4.4%	0.9%
Papua New Guinea	6.9%	6.0%	8.4%	2.2%
Samoa	6.3%	0.8%	5.2%	2.0%
Solomon Islands	7.1%	1.1%	7.3%	5.9%
Timor-Leste	0.7%	6.8%	13.5%	11.8%
Tonga	1.4%	3.6%	6.3%	1.2%
Vanuatu	4.3%	2.8%	0.9%	1.4%

deflation, **hyperinflation**, **inflation rate (rate of inflation)**, **stagflation**, **Fig. 24** (p. 67), **Fig. 50** (above), **Fig. 51** (above).

inflation rate (rate of inflation)

the rate of change in the increase in prices of goods and services, measured as the percentage increase of a price index such as the consumer price index (CPI). Inflation rate can be measured on a monthly, quarterly or annual basis. The example below is a calculation of the inflation rate over a three-month period. See **CPI**, **deflation**, **hyperinflation**, **inflation**, **stagflation**, **Fig. 50** (above), **Fig. 51** (above).

infrastructure [**in**-fruh-struhk-sher]
the network of services that enable the economy to function. It includes communications systems, roads, airports, shipping and harbours, energy and water production and distribution, hospitals and other essential services. Much of this infrastructure is provided and maintained by government.

inferior product
See **inferior good**.

inputs
the resources that are combined during the production process to produce outputs.

injunction [in-**juhngk**-shn]
a legal order that stops someone from doing something. For example, obtaining an injunction to stop a union from going on strike.

insider trading
the buying or selling of company shares to make a profit by people who have confidential information not available to the public. In many countries insider trading is restricted by law and by stock exchange regulations but is often very difficult to detect.

insolvency [in-**sol**-vuhn-see]
when a person or business is unable to pay their debts.

insolvent
when an individual or business is unable to pay debts as they become due.

instalment
one of a series of equal payments for goods or services, spread over a period of time. A usual method of payment for goods bought through hire purchase.

insurable interest [in-**shur**-uh-bull]
an insurance term. When taking out an insurance policy it must be shown that the policy holder (or the beneficiary) must stand to suffer a direct financial loss if the event against which the insurance cover is taken were to occur.

insurance [in-**shur**-uhns]

a method of protecting a person or firm against financial loss resulting from damage to, or theft of, personal and business assets (general insurance) and death or injury (life or accident insurance). The person or firm taking out the insurance pays amounts of money, called premiums, to the insurance company. The insurance company will pay out if losses are suffered by the policy holder. See **insurance company**.

insurance agent

See **insurance broker**.

insurance assessor

a person who estimates the loss when a claim is made on an insurance policy.

insurance broker

a person or firm that bring together clients seeking insurance and insurance companies that offer suitable policies. The broker receives a commission from the insurance company and assists the insured when a claim is made.

insurance company

a financial institution that provides insurance policies to protect individuals or firms against the risk of financial loss, in return for regular payment of premiums.

insurance cover

1. the situation against which the holder of an insurance policy is insured. For example, third-party property insurance insures against damage to other people's property such as their car or a building.
2. the amount covered under the policy. This is the maximum amount that can be paid out on a claim.

insurance extension

extra insurance cover, over and above a normal insurance policy, and for which an additional premium is paid. For example, insurance on buildings may not cover damage from floods or riots, and these risks will have to be specially written into the insurance policy for an additional premium.

insurance policy

a legal document that provides details of the terms and conditions of an insurance contract.

insurance premium

the specific amount paid, usually annually, to the insurer to provide the insurance cover detailed in an insurance policy.

insure [in-**shur**]

to take out an insurance policy.

insured [in-**shurd**]

the person or firm that takes out an insurance policy.

insurer [in-**shur**-er]

the insurance company.

intangible asset [in-**tan**-juh-bull]

an asset that has value but is not physical. Examples include copyrights, goodwill in a business, patents, trademarks and brand recognition. See **copyright**, **brand value**, **goodwill**, **patent**, **trademark**.

integration [in-ti-**gray**-shn]

See **horizontal integration**, **lateral integration**, **vertical integration**.

interdependence [in-ter-di-**pen**-duhns]

the relationship between individuals, firms or sectors in which each relies on the other. See **dependence**.

interest

1 the charge paid for the use of borrowed money, usually expressed as an annual percentage rate. Interest is calculated by either simple-interest calculation, or compound-interest calculation. See **compound interest**, **simple interest**, **Fig. 23** (p. 62).

2 the amount of ownership a stockholder has in a company, usually expressed as a percentage. For example, 'Mary has a 50% interest in the company'.

interest rate

the cost of borrowing money expressed as an annual percentage rate.

See **compound interest**, **interest**, **simple interest**, **Fig. 23** (p. 62).

interim dividend

[**in**-ter-uhm]

see **dividend**.

intermediate good

a good which is not a final good but is used in the production of final goods. Also called producer goods. Examples include fuel, natural resources and components. See **capital good**, **consumer good**, **producer good**.

internal audit

an 'in-house' audit of an organisation's records, procedures or systems. Unlike external audits, internal audits are normally conducted by the organisation's own employees or specialists engaged for the task. Internal audits are used to prevent fraud within the organisation and to ensure that the decisions of the board are being implemented.

internal finance

the ability of a company to finance its growth from retained profits. A company's net profits can be distributed to shareholders as dividends, used to finance growth or a mixture of both. See **dividends**, **retained profits**.

internal rate of return (IRR)

a method for evaluating whether a proposed project is financially desirable. The rate of discount that would need to be applied to make the net value of all cash flows from a project equal to zero. If the predicted IRR is less than the current rate of return in the securities market, then the firm may decide not to go ahead with the project and simply invest its retained profits in the market. See **Fig. 54** (p. 181).

internal revenue

[**rev**-uhn-yoo]

all monies collected by a government from domestic sources, such as income tax and taxes on activities such as gambling. Internal revenue does not include customs duties charged on imported goods. Also called inland revenue.

international accounting standards

internationally recognised accounting standards used by many countries, including Papua New Guinea, that do not have their own accounting standards.

International Finance Corporation (IFC)

a subsidiary of the World Bank that promotes private sector development, particularly in developing countries, through loans without government guarantees. Unlike the World Bank, the IFC charges market interest rates. See **World Bank**.

International Labour Organization (ILO)

an organisation set up by the United Nations to improve working conditions everywhere in the world.

International Monetary Fund (IMF) [mun-i-ter-ee]

an institution of the United Nations, which provides soft loans to countries to help them with their macroeconomic issues. See **soft loan**, **World Bank**.

international trade

the exchange of goods and services between countries through exports and imports. In 2012, the top ten older industrialised and newly industrialised countries accounted for over 50% of all international trade. See **Fig. 52** (below).

Figure 52 International trade of goods 2012

Country	*US$ billion*	*Share (%)*
United States	3882.7	10.58%
China	3867.1	10.54%
Germany	2575.5	7.02%
Japan	1684.7	4.59%
Netherlands	1247.8	3.40%
France	1243.8	3.39%
United Kingdom	1164.9	3.18%
South Korea	1067.5	2.91%
Italy	988.1	2.69%
Hong Kong	950.2	2.59%

Internet

a global network in which any computer can

communicate with any other computer, as long as they are both connected to the Internet. Connection to the Internet is usually through a landline or mobile telephone infrastructure. The Internet is used to exchange information through the World Wide Web, sending and receiving email and undertake e-commerce. See **e-commerce (ecommerce)**, **World Wide Web**.

Internet marketing

also called online marketing or advertising. Advertising and marketing using the World Wide Web and email. Internet marketing is used to support traditional types of advertising like radio, television, newspapers and magazines and also to attract consumers to online shopping sites. See **advertising**, **electronic commerce**, **Internet**, **online shopping**.

interview

a meeting of people, face-to-face, on the telephone, or online through video calling, especially one arranged with a person applying for a job in order to assess their experience, qualifications and ability to do the job.

intestate [in-**tes**-teyt]

a person who dies without having left a will.

in the red

being overdrawn and owing money to the bank. The phrase comes from the practice of using red ink to denote debt or losses on financial balance sheets.

inventory [**in**-vun-taw-ree]

list of items such as property, goods in stock, or the contents of a building.

investment

1 in economics, goods purchased to be used in the creation of wealth.
2 in finance, the purchase of assets such as shares or property, with the intention of receiving income in the future or their sale at a higher price.

investment bank

banks or divisions of banks that invest clients' capital

in creating capital for other corporations. They underwrite new debt and help corporations issue new shares and provide guidance to issuers regarding the issue and placement of stock. For a fee, they provide corporations with advice and assistance in mergers and acquisitions. Investment banks also trade securities for their own accounts. Neither investment banks nor merchant banks provide regular banking services to the general public. See **acquisition**, **merchant bank**, **merger**, **underwrite**.

investment banker

a person whose main business is raising capital for companies, governments and other entities, or who works in a large bank's division that is involved with these activities. Investment bankers may also provide other services to their clients, such as advice on mergers and acquisitions.

Investment Promotion Authority (IPA)

semi-government bodies in Papua New Guinea and Vanuatu, which promote and foster foreign investment in their home countries. In Papua New Guinea, the IPA issues the permits and licences necessary to carry out business in Papua New Guinea and registers companies, incorporated businesses, company names and trademarks.

investment trust

a company that invests shareholders' funds in a range of securities that are normally quoted on the stock exchange. Investors buy units (shares) in the trust and have their funds professionally managed and invested in a vide variety of companies.

investor

a person who purchases something with the aim of making profit from income, interest or resale.

invisible exports

services such as shipping and air transport, insurance, tourism and banking services that are provided to other countries. See **visible exports**.

invisible imports

services such as shipping and air transport, insurance, tourism and banking services that are provided by other countries. See **visible imports**.

invisible trade

refers to the export of services to, and import of services from, other countries. See **invisible exports**, **invisible imports**, **visible trade**.

invoice

1 a document containing a list of goods or services provided with their costs.
2 an itemised bill that is sent by a creditor to a debtor.

involuntary unemployment

workers who are willing to work for the going wage but are unable to find employment. See **voluntary unemployment**.

IOU

the pronunciation of 'I owe you'. A signed document acknowledging a debt and stating the amount of money owed.

IRR

see **internal rate of return**.

issued capital

the value of the total of a company's shares that have been allocated and held by shareholders. See **authorised capital**, **share**.

jettison

to voluntarily throw cargo overboard to lighten a ship that is in danger of sinking. See **general average**.

job

1 paid employment.
2 a task or series of tasks that need to be performed to produce a good or service.

job costing

calculating the cost of each job in a construction project or in the manufacture of a good.

job description

a formal, usually written, statement of the responsibilities of an employee.

job evaluation

an analysis of the value or worth of various jobs, so as to work out what people should be paid for doing different jobs.

job lot

a quantity of goods sold together at a reduced price to clear the goods from the business.

job-sharing

one full-time job shared between two part-time employees.

joint account

a bank account in the names of two or more people.

joint and several liability

a debt for which a number of people are jointly responsible. Any one of the people may be required to pay the debt in full if the others are unable to pay.

joint ownership

the ownership of property, land or a business by more than one person.

joint venture (JV)

a business arrangement in which two or more

parties agree to pool their resources for the purpose of accomplishing a specific task. Each of the parties in the JV is responsible for profits, losses and costs, but the JV is separate from the parties' other businesses. The gold mine in Pogera in the Enga Province of Papua New Guines in a joint venture between the Barrick Gold Corporation (95%) and the Government of Papua New Guinea (5%).

journal [jur-nl]

a book in which transactions are recorded before being transferred to the ledger. See **ledger**.

judgment creditor

a person or business to whom the court has directed a debtor to pay a debt.

judgment debtor

a person who has been ordered by a court to pay a debt.

junk bonds

a common term used to describe bonds that are high risk, that promise high returns but where there is serious doubt that the interest will be paid or the money returned at maturity. See **bond**.

junk mail

unwanted advertising or promotional material delivered through the mail. Junk mail sent as email is also called spam.

keyboard

the panel of keys that operates a computer, word processor or typewriter.

Keynesian economics

[**keen**-zee-uhn]

an approach to economics in which economists believe that markets react slowly to changes in equilibrium (especially to changes in prices) and therefore governments should sometimes put in place measures to get the economy back to equilibrium. See **allocation of resources**, **classical economics**, **economics**, **government intervention**, **market economy**.

key person

an important person in a business.

kickback

money paid to someone for providing help in a secret and dishonest business deal.

knock-for-knock

an agreement between insurance companies (of motor vehicles) under which each company agrees to meet the insurance claim of its insured. This agreement is made instead of going to court to establish blame for the accident and have the guilty party's insurance company meet the total claim.

labour

the physical and mental contributions of workers to production. In economics, labour is classified as one of the four main factors of production. See **factors of production**.

labour force

the number of people available for work. Includes people in employment plus people actively looking for work. Also called the working population.

labour-intensive

production that uses large amounts of labour and fewer other inputs. The proportion of labour used depends on both the type of production and the cost of labour. The young leaves used in the production of tea are hand-picked by women in Sri Lanka and machine-picked in Australia. Hairdressing, plumbing and clothing manufacture are examples of labour-intensive industries.

labour productivity

See **productivity**.

labour relations

see **industrial relations**.

labour supply

can be defined as the number of workers willing and able to work in a given occupation or industry for a given wage. There is usually a large number of workers available at a fairly low wage rate for low-skilled occupations. But there are usually fewer workers available for jobs that require specific skills and long periods of training, and they demand higher wage rates.

labourer

a person who does unskilled work.

laissez-faire [**les**-ey fair]

French for 'let do' or 'let it be'. Describes an economic environment in which dealings in the market between private parties are free from government restrictions, tariffs and subsidies, with only enough regulations to protect property rights. See **free market**.

land

property or real estate. In economics, land is classified as one of the four main factors of production and includes natural resources such as minerals and timber. See **custodians**, **customary land ownership**, **factors of production**, **natural resources**.

land groups and land registration

legislation in Papua New Guinea allows customary landowners to form Incorporated Land Groups (ILGs) and register parts of their land to be able to release it for development. One of the most critical issues facing Melanesian landowners is thatof how to become involved in the modern economy while at the same time maintaining the integrity of their land group and security over their landholdings. See **custodians**, **land ownership in Melanesia**.

land ownership in Melanesia

in most of Melanesia, land remains under customary title, controlled by clans and families. Land is group-owned and used by individuals for production. This customary ownership is recognised by the constitutions of Papua New Guinea, the Solomon Islands, Vanuatu and Timor Leste. Customary land cannot be sold, leased, mortgaged or disposed of except in accordance with custom. A relatively small proportion of customary land is either registered or alienated. See **alienated land**, **custodians**, **land groups and land registration**, **usufruct**.

land registration

See **custodians**, **land ownership in Melanesia**, **land groups and land registration**.

lateral integration

the amalgamation or joining together of firms who produce different goods at the same stage of production, such as two primary producers. This type of merger is also called a conglomerate merger, forming a conglomerate that produces many different products. Unilever, an international conglomerate that owns oil palm and coconut plantations in many Pacific countries, also has interests in transport and the manufacture of paint and plastics, and is one of the world's largest manufacturers of food and beverages.

law of demand

provided all other factors remain equal and nothing else changes (*ceteris paribus*), when prices rise the quantity demanded falls, and when prices fall the quantity demanded rises. See **ceteris paribus**, **demand**, **demand curve**, **law of supply**, **Fig. 31a** (p. 85).

law of supply

provided all other factors remain equal and nothing else changes (*ceteris paribus*), when prices rise the quantity supplied increases, and when prices fall the quantity supplied decreases. See **ceteris paribus**, **law of demand**, **supply**, **supply curve**, **Fig. 63a** (p. 245).

lawful

allowed by the law.

lawyer [**loy**-yer]

a person who is qualified by training and examination to advise people or firms on legal matters. See **barrister**, **solicitor**.

LIFO

acronym for *last in first out*. It is an accounting method that assumes that the most recently purchased items are sold first. See **stock**.

lead time

the time between placing an order and receiving the goods.

leaflet

a printed page, often folded, that contains information or advertising and is usually distributed free.

leakage

income or capital passing out of an economy. In economics it refers to income taken out of the circular flow as savings, taxation or money spent on imports. Leakages are sometimes called withdrawals. See **circular flow**, **Fig. 22** (p. 54).

lease

a legal document stating the conditions under which an owner (the lessor) agrees to rent a property or asset such as a motor vehicle to another party (the lessee). The lease guarantees the lessee use of the property for a specified period of time in return for regular rent payments to the lessor. See **lessee**, **lessor**.

lease back

selling property and then leasing it back from the purchaser.

leasehold land

land that is owned by the government or a landowner and then leased to a tenant for a fixed period of time. See **lease**.

leave

authorised time absent from work, such as annual leave, compassionate leave or sick leave. See **compassionate leave**, **sick leave**.

ledger

an accounting record in which the transactions of a business are entered direct or transferred from journals. Most ledgers are now maintained on computers.

legacy

money or property left to someone (a beneficiary) in a will.

legal

lawful, or allowed by the law.

legal expenses
money paid to a lawyer for legal advice or for court representation.

legal tender
the official medium of payment recognised by the laws of the country that can be used in exchange for goods, services and debt. The national currency is usually the legal tender of a country. Currencies like the US dollar and the euro are accepted as legal tender in many countries.

lend
to give someone a sum of money that is expected to be paid back, usually with interest.

least developed countries
term not in common use. See **developing economy (country)**.

less developed countries (LDCs)
term not in common use. See **developing economy (country)**.

lessee [les-**ee**]
a person who rents a property or other assets from its owner (the lessor) on a lease. See **lease**, **lessor**.

lessor [le-**sawr**]
a person who owns a property or other assets and rents it out to someone else (a lessee) on a lease. See **lease**, **lessee**.

let
another word for renting, usually used with renting a house, office or apartment.

letterhead
the printed letter form of a business, which includes the name, address, telephone, fax, email and other details of the company.

letter of credit
a document providing guaranteed payment before delivery of the goods or services. It is used in international trade. The exporter receives payment from a bank by producing the invoice for the goods or services before they are sent.

leverage [**lev**-er-ij]
to use borrowed capital to make an investment such as buying and selling stocks and shares. The investor expects that the profits made will be greater than the interest paid on the loan. Leverage can make large profits for the investor but it comes with greater risk. If the price of stocks and shares bought using leverage falls, the investor's loss is much greater than it would have been if the investment had not been leveraged. Leverage magnifies both gains and losses. See **long**, **short**, **options contract**.

levy [**lev**-ee]
1 a tax or charge such as a government tax on cigarettes or alcohol.
2 an additional payment for a specific purpose, required by members of a group such as a club or owners of apartments in a block. The club may need money to repay a debt or build a swimming pool, or the apartment block may need money to carry out major repairs.

liability
a debt owed by a business or an individual.

licence [**ly**-suhns]
1 a written authority to do something, such as sell liquor or drive a car.
2 to issue a licence.

licensee [ly-suhn-**see**]
a person who owns or holds a licence.

licensor [ly-suhn-**saw**]
a person or organisation who has the right to issue a licence.

lien [leen]
the right to hold a debtor's property until they have paid their debt in full.

life expectancy
the average length of time that people in a country are expected to live.

limited liability
a type of investment in which a shareholder of a company cannot lose more than what they have already invested. The investor or shareholder is not personally responsibility

for any debts that the company is unable to repay.

limit pricing

where the price of a product or service is set (usually lower than the cost of production) by a monopoly or oligopoly to discourage entry of competitors into a market. See **anti-competitive practices**, **monopoly**, **oligopoly**.

liquid assets

cash or assets that can be easily bought or sold. See **asset**.

liquidation [lik-wi-**dey**-shn]

the legal process by which a company is brought to an end, and the assets and property of the company sold or redistributed. Also called winding up. See **liquidator**.

liquidator [**lik**-wi-dey-ter]

a person appointed by the shareholders, creditors or the court, to liquidate or wind-up a company, sell off its assets, pay unsecured creditors with the proceeds of the sale and if any money is left, distribute it proportionally among the shareholder. See **asset**, **liability**, **liquidation**.

liquidity [li-**kwid**-i-tee]

1 the measure of whether a person or organisation has sufficient cash or assets that can be quickly converted to cash, to meet immediate and short-term liabilities.
2 in accounting, the ability of current assets to meet current liabilities.
3 a description of an asset such as gold or gilt-edge securities that can be easily bought and sold without affecting their price.

listed company

a limited liability company that offers its shares for sale to the public through a stock exchange.

loan

an amount of money lent or borrowed and is expected to be repaid at a future date, usually with interest.

local area network (LAN)

a network of computers in a company or organisation, connected by cable or radio signals to allow easy internal communications.

lockout

an action taken by employees during an industrial dispute to stop workers entering the workplace. See **industrial dispute**.

long (long-position)

1 the buying of a stock, commodity or currency, hoping that the asset will rise in value and could be sold at a profit. Investors often borrow money to buy shares. An investor who believes that prices will increase is called a bull. See **bull**, **short**.

2 the buying of an options contract. See **options contract**.

long run

a period of time long enough to have all factors of production vary. Also called the long term. See **short run**.

long service leave

a period of extra paid leave given to an employee after a long period of service.

long term

See **long run**.

loss

the opposite of profit in a business deal, or the annual result of the company's financial transactions.

loss adjuster

a person appointed by an insurance company to assess the amount of compensation that should be paid to someone making an insurance claim.

loss leader

a strategy in which a business offers goods at less than cost price to attract customers. The hope is that customers entering the store will either buy other goods or continue to buy the product in the future, leading to a profitable situation.

low geared

see **gearing**.

Luddites

workers in 19th-century England who destroyed machines which were saving labour and causing job losses. Nowadays it is a term used to describe people who are against or slow to adopt new technologies.

luxury [**luhk**-shuh-ree]
any good or service whose consumption rises more than proportionally to increases in income. Luxuries have an income elasticity of demand much greater than 1. Luxury goods are more expensive, better-quality, non-essential goods such as holidays and entertainment. Richer people spend a greater proportion of their income on luxuries than poorer people. See **elasticity**, **income elasticity of demand**, **inferior good**, **normal good**.

macroeconomic policy

government policies aimed at macroeconomic issues such as avoiding inflation, attaining full employment and maintaining economic growth. See **macroeconomics.**

macroeconomics

the branch of economics concerned with the study of overall economic issues such as the level of outputs and consumption, the levels of employment and the rates of inflation.

mail

letters and parcels sent by post.

mailing list

a database of names and addresses of people and businesses to whom advertising and other information such as price lists are regularly mailed. See **mail merge**.

mail merge

a computer process that is used to add names and addresses from a database to letters and envelopes. Used for example to send advertising to many different addresses.

managed floating exchange rate

a system by which a government tries to maintain the exchange rate of its currency. This is done by the government buying its own currency to prevent its value falling or selling currency to prevent it rising in value. Governments need to have large foreign exchange reserves to be able to undertake this. See **fixed exchange rate**, **floating exchange rate**, **foreign exchange reserves**.

management

1 the process of achieving the objectives of an organisation's goals by working with and

through people and other available resources.

2 the person or people who control and direct the affairs of a business or other organisation.

management accountant

the accountant who provides accounting information to management. This information is not made available to shareholders in a company.

management audit

a report on the performance of the management. This is different to the financial audit, which checks on the accuracy or otherwise of the financial results.

management by exception

checking on the performance of those sections of the business whose actual results show large differences from the budget.

management by objectives

a process of setting objectives for an organisation in which both management and employees agree to the objectives and understand what they need to do in order to achieve them.

management consultant

a person who reviews the current management practices of a business and advises on how to improve performance.

management information system (MIS)

a computer system that stores and provides information to help organise, evaluate and efficiently manage activities within a business.

manager

a person who is employed to control, organise and direct part or all of a business or organisation. Examples include a general manager, a marketing manager and a production manager.

managing director

a full-time manager who is also a director of the company.

managing partner

the person in a partnership who is also responsible for the management of the business.

manifest

a list of the cargo carried on a ship or an aircraft.

manufacture

the making of goods for use or sale using labour, machines, tools, raw materials and components.

margin

1 the gross profit margin is the difference between the cost price and the selling price of goods or services.
2 borrowed money used to purchase stocks, shares and other securities.

marginal

in economics the term marginal is used to mean something that has been added and was not there before. See **marginal cost**.

marginal costs

the additional cost (extra to total cost) necessary to produce each additional unit of a good or service. Given that fixed costs do not change with output, marginal costs are all variable costs. See **fixed costs**, **variable costs**.

marginal output

See **marginal physical product**.

marginal physical product (MPP)

(of a given input) the additional output that can be produced for each additional unit of the input, assuming that the quantities of all other inputs to production remain unchanged.

marginal product

See **marginal physical product**.

marine insurance

insurance for a ship and for goods carried by the ship.

mark-down

a reduction in the selling price of goods.

market

1 traditionally, a market is a physical place where people meet to buy and sell goods. In

economics the market is any situation that allows buyers and sellers to exchange goods, services or information.

2 all the people who want to buy or sell a specific product or service, for example the housing market.

market demand

the total of the demand for a specific good or service at a given time at each of different prices. See **demand**, **demand curve**, **market demand schedule**, **market demand curve**, **Fig. 31a** (p. 85).

market demand curve

See **demand curve**, **demand schedule**, **market demand**, **Fig. 31a** (p. 85).

market demand schedule

See **demand curve**, **demand schedule**, **market demand**, **Fig. 31a** (p. 85), **Fig. 32** (p. 85).

market economic system

See **market economy**.

market economy

a theoretical economic system in which all decisions regarding investment, production and supply are made according to the laws of supply and demand. The assumption behind this system is that the market itself can make sure that resources are allocated efficiently and equally without government intervention or central planning. Pure market economies do not exist. There is some level of government intervention in the economy. Even with this intervention, free market economies sometimes fail. See **allocation of resources**, **centrally planed economy**, **economic system**, **free-market economy**, **Keynesian economics**, **market failure**.

market equilibrium

See **equilibrium**, **Fig. 42** (p. 109).

market failure

a breakdown in the free market due to inefficient and unequal allocation of goods and services. In the years after 2007 the world experienced the Global Financial Crisis (GFC). In the USA many banks failed, the price of stocks decreased and the value of houses fell sharply. This was an example of failure in the market system. Monopolies, a lack of information and understanding, self interest and negative externalities, the production of more goods for those who can pay more, and the failure to provide public goods and services all contribute to market failure. See **allocation of resources**, **Keynesian economics**, **monopoly**, **negative externalities**, **public goods**.

market forces

the economic factors that affect the demand for, the availability of and the price of a good or service in a free market.

market leader

the business that sells most of a particular product in a country or the world.

market price

the current price at which a good or service can be bought or sold. In economics, the market price is determined by supply and demand and will change until equilibrium is reached. See **equilibrium**.

Independent Public Business Corporation (IPBC)

an independent entity established under an Act of Parliament to hold the majority of state-owned commercial assets in trust for the State of Papua New Guinea.

market oriented

a company or organisation that tries to produce and market products and services that meet the desires and demands of customers.

market research

studies carried out by companies to identify the needs of buyers and the extent to which these needs are being satisfied.

market share

the percentage of the total sales of a good or service that a company is achieving in the market. If a company is selling half of all the particular good or service bought in the market it has a market share of 50%.

market supply

the total of a specific good or service supplied in the market by all producers at each price over a specific period of time. See **supply**, **individual supply**, **supply schedule**, **Fig. 63a** (p. 245), **Fig. 64** (p. 246).

market supply curve

See **individual supply**, **supply**, **supply curve**, **supply schedule**, **Fig. 63a** (p. 245), **Fig. 64** (p. 246).

marketing

the activities undertaken by a business to promote the sales of its goods and services. Marketing includes advertising and market research. See **advertising**, **market research**.

marketing manager

the person who is in charge of the marketing of a company's goods and services. See **marketing**.

mark-up

the amount added to the cost price of goods to calculate the selling price. This is often done by adding a percentage to the cost price. For example, if a good with a cost price of K4 is marked up by 50%, the selling price would be K6.

mass production

the making of large quantities of identical goods by using machines. Mass production allows producers to sell their goods at a low price and thus produce high sales.

master copy

the original copy of a document.

maternity leave

paid time off work, allowed under law, to a mother for a period before and after the birth of her child.

MBA

abbreviation of *Master of Business Administration*, a higher university degree in business studies.

means of production

See **capital goods**.

media

various forms of communication such as television, radio, newspapers and the Internet, which businesses use to advertise and promote their products.

medium of exchange

one of the functions of money whereby people exchange goods and services for money and in turn use money to obtain other goods and services. See **functions of money**, **money**.

meeting

a group of people getting together to discuss, exchange views on and make decisions on matters on the agenda. See **agenda**.

memo [**mem**-o]

abbreviation for *memorandum*. See **memorandum**.

memorandum

[mem-uh-**ran**-duhm]

1 a short note to help remember something.
2 a record or written statement.
3 a written message sent from one employee of a company to other employees.

memorandum of association

a document that describes the composition of a company and its objectives. A memorandum of association is required in some countries before a company can be incorporated and in others has been replaced by a Constitution.

merchandise

[**mur**-chuhn-dyz]

goods for sale.

merchant bank

similar to an investment bank except that merchant banks invest their own capital while investment banks operate on behalf of clients. Most modern banking institutions have elements of both, but increasingly regulations require banks to 'ring fence' or separate their investment banking from their other banking activities. Neither investment nor merchant banks provide regular banking services to the general public. See **investment bank**.

merger

the combining of two or more companies into one.

merit goods

goods and services provided free by governments for the benefit of all members of society. Education is an example of a merit good. See **non-rival goods**, **non-excludable products**, **public goods**, **public service**.

microcredit

the provision of very small loans for poor or low-income individual or group borrowers with little or no collateral. See **microfinance**, **unbanked**.

microeconomics

the branch of economics concerned with the study of the economies of individuals, households, companies and industries. It looks at how and why individuals and families make choices on what to buy and how producers decide on what and how much to produce and what prices to charge. See **macroeconomics**.

microfinance

financial services such as credit, savings, insurance, money transfers, and other financial products for poor or low-income individuals or groups. The services are provided by businesses and organisations called microfinance institutions. Mobile money with a smartphone could make microfinance more efficient and widely available. The term microfinance is often confused with microcredit. See **microcredit**, **mobile banking**, **mobile money**, **unbanked**.

middleman

a person who buys goods from the producer and sells them to the retailer.

migration

the movement of people between regions or countries. The movement into a country is called immigration and the movement out of a country is called emigration.

minimum wages
the minimum wage that is legally allowed to be paid.

minority interest
a holding of less than 50% of shares in a company. A holder of a minority interest is unable to control the company.

minutes
an official written record of a meeting. The minutes must be confirmed as being correct at the next meeting. The minutes must be corrected if members do not agree that they correctly represent what took place at the meeting.

mission statement
a statement of the aims and purpose of an organisation.

mixed economy
an economy that has a mixture of free markets and some government control and intervention. See **allocation of resources**, **centrally planed economy**, **Keynesian economics**.

mixed economy system
See **mixed economy**.

mobile application
also called mobile app. An Internet application that runs on smartphones and other mobile devices. Mobile applications connect the user to specific Internet services such as mobile banking.

mobile banking
a system that allows customers of a bank or other financial institution to conduct financial transactions using a mobile application on a smartphone. See **mobile applications**, **smartphone**, **unbanked**.

mobile money
also called mobile wallet. The use of a mobile application on a smartphone to pay for items at stores, transfer funds between banks or accounts, deposit or withdraw funds, or pay bills. Mobile money will help people in rural areas of the Pacific, who currently have

no access to banks, to better manage their daily lives and improve their livelihoods. See **e-commerce (ecommerce)**, **mobile banking**, **mobile payments**, **near field communication**.

mobile payments

instead of paying with cash, cheque, or credit cards, a consumer can use a mobile application on a smartphone with near field communication (NFC) technology to pay for goods or services at the business place of the supplier. Common in Japan and South Korea, this technology is slowly increasing in the rest of the world. See **e-commerce (ecommerce)**, **mobile application**, **mobile banking, mobile money**.

model

a simplified system that economists use to represent some aspect of real economics. The real world of economics is large, has many variables, is complicated and cannot be simply explained. A model concentrates on selected variables, showing the relationships between them, and ignores everything else. In this way, one variable can be changed to study the effect of that change on another variable. See **ceteris paribus**.

modem [**moh**-duhm]

an electronic device that allows one computer to send information to another computer through standard phone lines. Modems are essential for connecting computers to the World Wide Web and Internet. See **Wi-Fi**, **wireless router**.

monetary policy [**muhn**-i-ter-ee]

the control of interest rate and money supply by governments and their central banks, to influence the economy.

money

a means of payment and storage of wealth either as physical banknotes and coins or as computer or book entries such as in bank deposits. See **functions of money**,

medium of exchange, **store of value**.

money-lender

a person or business that lends money to others who pay interest. The interest charged is usually at a higher rate than that of a bank. Individuals in many Pacific countries make short-term loans to others at very high interest rates. See **usury**.

money market

a market involved in the lending and borrowing of money for short periods of time, such as overnight. The money market usually deals in very large transactions and the main participants are banks and other financial institutions.

money supply

the total amount of money that exists in the economy of a country.

monopoly [muh-**nop**-uh-lee]

only one seller in the market. Monopolies are characterised by an absence of competition and often result in high prices. Many countries have laws and regulations against anti-competitive practices to protect free markets from being dominated by a single supplier. Monopolies are unavoidable in some circumstances, such as when a business or individual is granted a patent on a new invention, giving it, in effect, a monopoly on a product for a set period of time. See **anti-competitive practices**, **barriers to market entry**, **patent**.

mortgage [**mawr**-gij]

a loan taken by an individual or company (the mortgagor) to purchase an asset such as a house, a building, or shares. The ownership of the asset remains with the lender (the mortgagee) until the loan is repaid in full. At that point the ownership of the asset passes back to the mortgagor.

mortgagee [mawr-guh-**jee**]

the lender of the money in a mortgage.

mortgagor [mawr-guh-**jor**]

the borrower of the money in a mortgage.

motion

a formal suggestion that is discussed and voted on at a meeting. If the motion is passed, it becomes a resolution.

motor vehicle insurance

sometimes called comprehensive motor vehicle insurance. This provides insurance cover for the car, the driver, the passengers, and people and assets outside the car, such as other cars and people in them, pedestrians and property. Insurance covering only people and assets outside the car is compulsory and is known as third party personal insurance. See **insurance**, **third party personal insurance**, **third party property insurance**.

mouse

a hand-operated electronic device attached to a computer that when moved moves the cursor (pointer) on a computer screen. Most portable computers now have a small inbuilt touch-sensitive pad called a touchpad. By moving a finger along the touchpad, the pointer on the display screen is moved.

multinational

a company that operates in several countries.

mutual fund

a pool of funds collected from many investors for the purpose of investing in securities such as stocks, bonds, money market instruments and similar assets. Mutual funds are operated by money managers, who invest the fund's capital and attempt to produce capital gains and income for the fund's investors. Mutual funds give small investors access to professional management and a range of investments that would be difficult to access with a small amount of capital. See **hedge fund**.

national debt

the total amount of money that a government owes to creditors. National debt is the accumulated results of budget deficits. See **budget deficit**.

national income

the total of all income received by the residents of a country in a year.

national product

the total value of all goods and services produced in a country in a year. Also called Gross National Product (GNP).

National Provident Fund

compulsory saving scheme for employees established by Acts of Parliament in several Pacific countries. Both employees and employers make regular contributions to the fund with the aim of providing retirement lump sums or pensions for employees. Severe financial losses caused by fraud, corruption and mismanagement of the fund in Papua New Guinea caused a collapse in 2000, leading to members losing half their savings.

nationalised industry

an industry whose ownership has been taken over by the government. See **privatisation**.

natural monopoly

a situation in which one firm, because of its access to a raw material, advanced technology, or other factors, can supply a market's entire demand for a good or service at a price lower than any other firms can. Public utilities are usually considered to be natural monopolies. See **monopoly**.

natural person

in legal terms, a natural person is a real human being, as opposed to a legal person, which may, for example, be a company or an organisation.

natural resources

everything on, under and above the land, rivers and seas. The 'gifts of nature' that include land, trees, fish, petroleum and mineral deposits, the fertility of soil, climatic conditions, crops and other raw materials. In economics, natural resources are included under the factor on production called land. See **factors of production**, **land**, **renewable resources**, **non-renewable resources**.

near field communication (NFC)

a technology used in mobile payment systems. When making payments the smartphone or credit card is placed a few inches from a supplier's NFC terminal to establish radio communication between the two. Funds are then transferred from the customer's bank account directly into the bank account of the supplier. See **mobile payments**.

near money

any easily sellable (liquid) asset other than cash which can be very quickly converted to cash. See **liquid asset**.

needs

in economics, a need is something that is necessary for a person to survive and function in society. Food, water, clothing, shelter and air are physical needs, while love, a feeling of security and approval are mental needs. A lack of these can result in either physical or mental illness and even death. See **wants**.

negative externalities

effects of economic activities that result in costs for people other than the buyers or sellers (third parties). Many negative externalities are related to environmental pollution caused by the production process. Greenhouse gases and water pollution are examples of negative externalities. See **climate change**, **externalities**, **external costs of production**, **global** warming, greenhouse gas, positive externalities.

negotiable

[ni-**goh**-shuh-buhl]

1 an agreement or situation that is open to discussion or change.
2 the price of a good or security that is not firmly established.
3 a good or security whose ownership is easily transferable from one party to another.

negotiable instrument

a written order such as a cheque that unconditionally promises to pay a named individual a fixed sum of money on demand or at a certain time and can be transferred from one person to another.

negotiate [ni-**goh**-shee-eyt]

to try to reach an agreement through discussion.

negotiation

[ni-goh-shee-**ey**-shn]

See negotiate.

net

the amount remaining after all deductions have been made. For example, the net profit is the profit that is made after all expenses have been deducted. See net income, net profit.

net advantages of a job

the total benefits of a job including wages and other cash payments, fringe benefits or perks, promotion prospects, job satisfaction, job security and pleasant working conditions. See fringe benefits, perks.

net asset value

the difference between a company's assets and liabilities. A measure of the total value of the company.

net asset value per share

the difference between a company's assets and liabilities divided by the number of ordinary (or equity) shares. A measure of the value of each share in the company.

net income

the amount of income received after deduction of tax.

net loss

the amount of loss incurred when total expenses are

greater than the total of sales and other forms of income such as interest received on deposits and investments.

net national product (NNP)

the value of the incomes received from the factors of production owned by residents of the country whether the production in undertaken domestically or abroad, less the value of depreciation of capital equipment (capital consumption). NNP does not include the income from factors of production operating domestically but owned by non-residents (foreign citizens). See **capital consumption**, **gross national income**.

net present value

the sum of the annual expected present value return from an asset over the life of the asset. The present day value of returns are calculated by discounting net annual income by the required rate of return. For example, if the required rate of return is 20% then the net annual income is discounted by 20% in the first year and a further 20% for each of the following years. This sum of these figures is then compared with the original amount invested in the asset. For the investment in the asset to be financially acceptable, the net present value must equal to or greater than the original investment. See **internal rate of return**, **required rate of return**, **Fig. 54** (p. 181).

net profit

total revenue less the cost of doing business, depreciation, interest, taxes and other expenses. See **gross profit**.

net realisable value

an accounting method for calculating the worth of assets. The net realisable value of an item as calculated is its estimated sale price less selling costs such as repairs, disposal and commissions.

Figure 54 Checking net present value

Calculating net present value after 5 years on an investment of $175,000 with an estimated return of $60,000 a year. The required rate of return is 20%. The expected returns are discounted by 20% each year to convert them to present value. The table below shows the discount factor and the present value of each annual return.

Year	*Return*	*20% Discount Factor*	*Present Value of Return*
1	60,000	1/1.20 = 0.8333	60,000 × 0.8333 = 50,000
2	60,000	0.8333/1.20 = 0.6944	60,000 × 0.6944 = 41,667
3	60,000	0.6944/1.20 = 0.5787	60,000 × 0.5787 = 34,722
4	60,000	0.5787/1.20 = 0.4822	60,000 × 0.4822 = 28,935
5	60,000	0.4822/1.20 = 0.4018	60,000 × 0.4018 = 24,113
net present value after 5 years			**179,437**

The net present value of 179,437 is, after five years, greater than the initial investment of 175,000. The investment is therefore financially acceptable.

net worth

the amount by which the assets exceed the liabilities of a business or individual. See **asset**, **liability**.

no claims bonus

the reduction in annual premium for motor vehicle insurance received by a person or firm that has not made a claim in the previous year.

nominate

to put someone's name forward for election to a position in a club or association such as chairman, secretary or treasurer.

non-current asset

sometimes referred to as a fixed asset, such as motor vehicles, office equipment, buildings. Non-current assets are used over a long period of time to make profit in abusiness. See **current assets**.

non-current liabilities

a liability that is required to be paid after at least a year from the date of the balance sheet. Liabilities that have to be paid within a year are called current liabilities. See **current liability**.

non-durables

consumer goods expected to last less than three years. See **consumer durables**.

non-excludable goods

also called collective goods or public goods. Public goods or services that are provided by government, which are the same for everyone and are difficult to stop individuals using them. Examples include police protection, national defence and free to air television. See **excludable goods**, **merit goods**, **non-rival goods**, **public goods**.

non-excludable resource

resources that can be used by everyone. Examples include the air we breathe and fish in the sea. See **non-excludable products**, **non-rival goods**, **public goods**.

non-governmental organisation (NGO)

any nonprofit, voluntary group organised on a local, national or international level. NGOs perform a variety of service and humanitarian functions and some are organised around specific issues, such as human rights, environment or health. See **nonprofit**.

non-price competition

competition in which producers use factors such as packaging, delivery, or customer service rather than price to increase demand for their products.

nonprofit

organisation that does not distribute any net profits to individuals such as members, officers, directors, or trustees. The organisation may pay some of these individuals for services rendered and goods provided while others may provide services on a voluntary basis. See **non-governmental organisation (NGO)**.

non-renewable resources

also called finite resources. Resources that are not capable of being replaced in normal human time frames. Once used, a non-renewable resource is gone forever. Examples of non-renewable resources include minerals in the Earth's crust and fossil fuels such as oil and coal. See **renewable resources**.

non-rival goods

public goods that can be used at the same time by many users and not reduce in quantity or quality. Examples include street lighting, parks and the Internet. See **rival goods**.

non-tradeable good or service

good or service that is produced for the local market, for purchase with local currency, and does not compete in the global marketplace. The classic example given is a haircut. See **tradeable good or service.**

normal good

good whose demand increases as consumer incomes increase. They have a positive income elasticity of demand. Most goods other than inferior goods are normal goods. Normal goods include necessities which have positive income elasticity of demand of less than 1. See **income elasticity of demand**, **inferior good**, **luxuries**.

normal profit

just enough profit to keep the producer in business.

not negotiable

written between parallel lines on a cheque meaning that the cheque can only be paid into the account of the person whose name appears on the cheque. See **crossed cheque**.

null and void

having no legal effect and being invalid.

occupation
the type of work a person does.

occupational hazard
the risks in a particular type of work, such as back problems for workers lifting heavy articles.

oddment
an item that is sold cheaply because it is one of the last few of a line of goods.

offer
1 the price at which a party says it is willing to buy or sell an asset from/to another party. An offer is the first step in making a contract of sale or purchase. The offer may or may not be accepted.
2 to make an asset available for sale, such as to offer shares to investors.

offeree [off-uh-**ee**]
the person who receives an offer.

offeror [**off**-uh-rer]
the person who makes an offer.

offline
not connected to the Internet or a network of computers or other devices. The term is frequently used to describe someone who is temporarily disconnected from the Internet. See **Internet**, **online**.

oil
a fossil fuel that is the major source for energy in the world. Although it is a finite non-renewable resource that will some day run out, the world's oil reserves have not yet been fully explored. See **fossil fuel**.

oligopoly [ol-i-**gop**-uh-lee]
a situation in which a particular market is controlled by a small group of companies serving many buyers, with high barriers to entry, making it difficult for new firms to enter the market.

See **collusive oligopoly**, **monopoly**.

on approval
goods that may be returned if they are not suitable.

on demand
to ask for with proper authority, such as to ask for immediate payment of a debt.

online
connected to the Internet or a network of computers or other devices. The term is frequently used to describe someone who is currently connected to the Internet. See **Internet**, **offline**.

online bank
bank that does not have offices and branches and works completely through the Internet. Because they have lower overheads, online-only banks often offer consumers higher interest rates on deposits and lower fees and interest rates on loans.

online banking
also called Internet banking. A system allowing individuals to perform banking activities through the Internet. Some online banks are traditional banks which also offer online banking, while others are online only and have no physical presence. See **online bank**.

online shopping
also called online retailing. A form of electronic commerce that allows consumers to buy goods or services from a seller over the Internet. The consumer visits the seller's website, selects what they want to buy from the various goods or services available, and makes an electronic payment. See **e-commerce (ecommerce)**.

o.n.o.
acronym for *or near offer*. For example, a motor vehicle may be advertised for sale at K10 000 o.n.o. This allows potential buyers to make an offer less than the advertised price. The decision to sell remains with the seller. Also written *ono* and *ONO*.

online transaction

See **electronic commerce**.

OPEC

Organization of Petroleum Exporting Countries. A cartel of oil-producing countries that work together to manage the export of their crude oil to the rest of the world. Because of their ability to adjust production levels, they can influence the price of oil. See **cartel**.

open cheque

a cheque that is not crossed which can be cashed by anyone who takes it to the bank. See **crossed cheque**, **not negotiable**.

open economy

an economy that conducts transactions, including the trade in goods and services, the transfer of capital and information and the migration of labour, with the rest of the world. Most economies are open to some of these forms of contact but few are open to all. See **closed economy**.

open market

a market in which prices are determined by supply and demand with no barriers to entry and no trading restrictions.

open position

a situation in which a trader in securities and commodities who has entered into futures contracts to sell items not held and hedged by contracts to buy, faces a loss if the market rises. Similarly, a trader who has entered into futures contracts to buy without hedging by contracts to sell is at risk of a loss if the market falls. See **hedging**, **futures contracts**, **options contract**.

operating loss

a situation in which operating expenses are greater than operating income. It excludes such items as dividends and interest received.

operating profit

a situation in which operating income is greater than operating expenses.

It excludes such items as dividends and interest received.

opportunity cost

a direct result of making a choice. The opportunity cost is the difference between the option not chosen and the option chosen. For example, if a student decides to go to university rather than go straight into the work force the opportunity cost for her decision is the money she would have earned if she went straight to work. Similarly, if a farmer decides to grow sweet potatoes instead of English potatoes the opportunity cost would be the money he would have earned if he had decided to grow English potatoes. See **choice**, **scarcity**.

options contract

a contract that gives an investor the right to buy or sell a share at a given price, known as the strike price. The investor is required to pay a non-refundable premium for the right. For example, investor 'X' believes that the price of a stock will rise from its current price of K40 to a level nearing K100. Rather than purchasing the stock itself, she can purchase a call option from investor 'Y' for a premium price of, say, K4 a share to buy the shares at a strike price of K75. If the stock does rise to K100, investor 'X' has the right to buy the shares for K75 each and make a profit of K25 per share on the contract, minus the premium K4. If the share does not reach K75 then investor 'X' can decide to not exercise her right to buy and simply lose her K4 premium. See **call**, **derivative**, **put**.

option to purchase (property)

a contract that is purchased for a price that gives the right (but not the obligation) to buy a property, within a certain time, for a specified amount, and subject to specified conditions. The option may or may not be taken up. As with the premium paid in an options contract , the money is lost if the property is not bought. See **options contract**.

order

a request to supply goods or services.

order cheque

a cheque made out to a person or business with the words 'or order' after the payee's name. The payee may write on the back of the cheque authorising it to be paid to someone else. This is then called an endorsed cheque. See **endorse**, **payee**.

ordinary share

the main type of share in companies. Called common stock in the US. Holders of ordinary shares receive a share in any distributed dividends and are entitled to vote at any meetings. See **share**.

organisation

a group of people who share a purpose or interest, such as a business, political party, government department or charity.

original

the first document produced from which copies may be made.

out of stock

not currently having certain goods for sale. See **stock**.

output

the goods or services that are produced using a combination of factor inputs. See **factor inputs**.

outstanding

unpaid.

outstanding liability

an amount of money owed by an organisation.

outstanding revenue

an amount of money owed to an organisation.

outsourcing

buying services and finished or intermediate goods from outside suppliers, often based in high-skill, low-cost countries, rather than producing them within the company. A company will outsource either because it is more cost effective or because the outside sources have specialised technical skills not available within the company. See **call centre**, **cost minimisation**.

overcharge

an invoice made out for an amount higher than the agreed price, either because of a mistake or due to a misunderstanding.

overdraft

a negative balance in a bank account. The customer owes the bank money. See **bank overdraft**.

overdrawn

to have drawn more money out of a bank account that what was actually in the account. The customer owes the bank money.

overheads

the expenses of a business that are necessary to run a business. They include such items as rent, salaries, light, power, administrative expenses and depreciation. They are sometimes referred to as indirect expenses because they cannot be directly costed to a particular production process. See **indirect expenses**.

overtime

work done in addition to normal working hours and usually paid for at special overtime rates.

overtime rates

hourly rates paid for overtime work. These are usually time and a half rates, meaning 1.5 times the ordinary rate, and sometimes double time rates.

overtrading

where a company carries on business on a scale too large for its financial capacity.

ownership

the legal right to possess, use and dispose of an asset.

ozone layer [**oh**-zohn]

a layer of the atmosphere between 15 km and 50 km above the Earth's surface, where oxygen is converted to ozone by high-energy ultraviolet (UV) radiation. Most of the UV radiation from the Sun is absorbed by the ozone layer, therefore protecting living things on the Earth. Increased UV is known to cause skin and eye cancer in humans and animals. Several major economic crops including wheat, rice, barley, oats, corn and soybeans are particularly vulnerable to increased UV. In the 1980s it was discovered that holes were appearing in the ozone layer, particularly over the north and south poles. It is thought that these holes are being caused by gases called chlorofluorocarbons. Some refrigerators and cans of aerosol spray contain chlorofluorocarbons. International agreement to control CFC emissions was reached in 1987 in what is called the Montreal Protocol. See **externalities**, **negative externalities**, **pollution**.

p.a.

abbreviation for the Latin phrase *per annum*, meaning 'each year'.

Pacific Island Countries Trade Agreement (PICTA)

an initiative of the Pacific Islands Forum to establish a free-trade agreement between Forum countries that will remove tariffs on most goods by 2021. See **free trade**, **free trade agreement**, **free trade zone**, **Pacific Islands Forum**.

Pacific Islands Forum

an inter-governmental organisation whose main aim is to improve the economic and social well-being of the people of the South Pacific. Formally called the South Pacific Forum, the organisation changed its name in 1999 and expanded its membership to include both north and south Pacific nations. Military and police forces as well as civilian personnel of Forum states, chiefly Australia and New Zealand, have recently been part of regional peacekeeping operations in other member states such as in the Solomon Islands (2003), Nauru (2004–2009), and Tonga (2006). As well as its role in harmonising regional positions on various political and policy issues, the Forum Secretariat has technical programs in economic development, transport and trade. See **Pacific Island Countries Trade Agreement (PICTA)**.

Pacific Islands Forum Fisheries Agency (FFA)

an intergovernmental agency whose main role is to help countries sustainably manage their fishery resources, especially of tuna, within their 200-mile Exclusive Economic Zones (EEZs). FFA also deals with fishing vessel registration, and the surveillance and control of illegal and unknown fishing. See **Exclusive Economic Zone (EEZ)**.

paid up capital
the value of the total number of shares purchased by all shareholders of a company.

paid up policy
a life assurance policy in which, by arrangement between the insurance company and the insured person, no more regular cash payments of premiums have to be made. The ongoing premiums are deducted from the final cash value of the policy. When the insured person dies, the payout will be the original benefit minus the value of unpaid premiums.

paid up share
a share whose value has been fully paid.

pallet
a wooden or metal frame on which goods can be stored or transported.

panic buying
a rush to buy goods because consumers believe there will be a shortage of them.

paper loss
an estimate of the loss that would be incurred if an asset that has lost value is sold. The 'paper loss' is calculated by subtracting the current value of the asset from its original cost.

paper profit
an estimate of the profit that would be made if an asset that has increased in value is sold. The 'paper profit' is calculated by subtracting the original cost of the asset from its current value.

para
abbreviation for *paragraph*.

parent company
see **holding company**.

pareto optimal [pah-**re**-taw **op**-tuh-muhl]
optimal is the Latin word for 'best'. Vilfredo Pareto (1848–1923) was an Italian economist. The phrase describes a situation in which resources have been allocated in the most efficient manner possible. It is a situation in which it is impossible to make

one individual better off without making at least one individual worse off.

particular person call

a telephone call that goes through the operator, for connection to a particular person. The charge for the call, apart from a flat fee, does not commence until the particular person to whom the call is being made comes on to the line. Also called person-to-person call.

partner

a member of a partnership.

partnership

a legally established business owned by two or more individuals. The owners share all profits of the business and are personally responsible for any debts that the company is unable to repay.

Partnership Act

the Act of Parliament that governs partnerships.

partnership agreement

written agreement between two or more individuals who join as partners to form and carry on a for-profit business. The agreement describes the nature of the business, the capital contributed by each partner, their rights and responsibilities, and how the profits will be shared.

part-owner

someone who owns something jointly with others.

part time worker

an employee who works for less than the number of hours per week that a full-time worker does. See **job-sharing**.

party

a person or group of people that takes part in a negotiation or is involved in a legal agreement.

par value

also called the face value. It is the value of a share when it was first issued. This is not the market value of the share, which is the value at which the share is being traded on the stock exchange. See **share**.

pass book
a book that records all deposits and withdrawals from a bank account.

password
a secret word, phrase or series of numbers that must be used to gain admission to information. For example, passwords are used to give an individual access to their computer or email account, to an Internet site, or to their bank account online or at an ATM machine. Regularly changing passwords provides extra security.

patent [**pay**-tent]
a government licence that gives the holder the sole right to make, use or sell an invention and stops others from copying it. Patents are usually valid for a set period of time. See **copyright**, **monopoly**.

patent office [**pay**-tent]
a government office that issues patents. See **patent**.

pay
money paid to an employee for work done.

payable
the amount of money that is owing.

pay as you earn (PAYE)
tax is deducted from an employee's earnings by the employer each pay period and forwarded to the tax authority.

payback period
the estimated length of time that it takes for the cash receipts from an investment, such as dividends and interest, to equal the initial cost of an investment.

PAYE
acronym for *pay as you earn*. See **pay as you earn**.

payee
the person to whom money is being paid and especially to whom a cheque is made payable.

payment
the amount of money being paid.

pay packet
1 an envelope containing an employee's wages.
2 the amount of money a person earns.

pay phone
a public telephone that requires the user to pay with coins or a card to make a telephone call. See **phone card**.

payroll
the list of employees showing their gross earnings, tax deducted, other deductions and their net pay. It is usually prepared each fortnight.

pay scale
the various levels of wages paid in an organisation or profession.

pay slip
a small sheet of paper given to employees when they are paid showing their gross wages, tax and other deductions and the net amount paid.

PBX
abbreviation for *private branch exchange*. See **private branch exchange**.

PC
abbreviation for *personal computer*. See **personal computer**.

pension
a regular payment paid:

- by an employer to a former employee who has retired or to their widowafter they have died.
- by the state to people who have reached a certain age or who cannot work because of an injury or other disability.

pension fund
regular contributions made by the employee and employer during the employee's working life that are invested to provide the employee with a pension when they retire. See **pension**.

per annum
each year. See **p.a.**

percentage change

the change in a variable expressed as a percentage of its original value.

perfect competition

a situation where:

- there are large numbers of buyers and sellers;
- there are no barriers to new producers entering the market;
- consumers get what they want;
- goods and services offered by different producers are of similar quality; and
- both producers and consumers have access to information and knowledge about the market and prices.

See **imperfect competition**, **perfect market**.

perfect market

a situation where there is perfect competition and no one producer or consumer influences the price charged for goods and services. See **perfect competition**.

perfectly elastic

a theoretical situation in which the smallest change in one variable will cause an infinitely large change in another. See **perfectly elastic demand**, **perfectly elastic supply**, **Fig. 55** (below).

Figure 55 Perfect elasticity

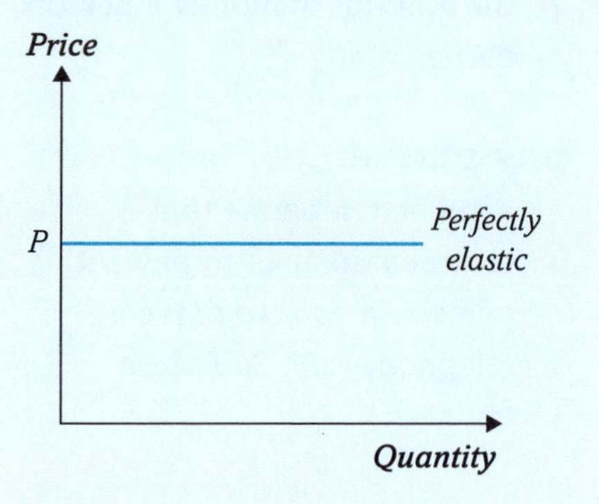

perfectly elastic demand

a theoretical situation in which even the smallest rise in price will result in zero demand and even the smallest reduction in price will result in infinite demand. Elasticity is infinite and the demand curve a horizontal straight line. See **elasticity of demand**, **perfect elasticity**, **Fig. 55** (above).

perfectly elastic supply

a theoretical situation in which even the smallest reduction in price will result in zero supply and even the smallest rise in price will result in infinite supply. Elasticity is infinite and the supply curve a horizontal straight line. See **elasticity of supply**, **perfect elasticity**, **Fig. 55** (p. 196).

perfectly inelastic

situation in which one variable will not be affected by any change in another. Elasticity is zero. See **elasticity**, **perfectly inelastic demand**, **perfectly inelastic supply**, **Fig. 56** (below).

Figure 56 Perfect inelasticity

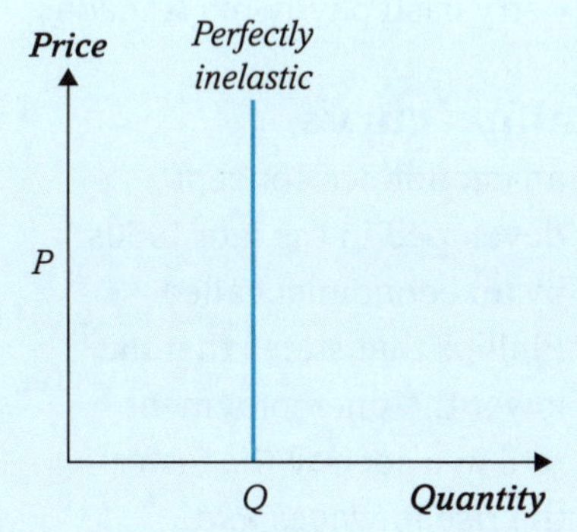

perfectly inelastic demand

situation in which the quantity demanded of a good or service will not be affected by any change in price. Elasticity is zero and the demand curve is a vertical straight line. See **perfect inelasticity**, **Fig. 56** (below).

perfectly inelastic supply

situation in which the quantity supplied of a good or service will not be affected by any change in price. Elasticity is zero and the supply curve is a vertical straight line. See **perfect inelasticity**, **Fig. 56** (below).

performance appraisal

a meeting between an employee and a manager to discuss the quality of the employee's work, and areas for future progress.

perks

an abbreviation of the word *perquisite* which means benefits an employee receives in addition to a wage or salary. Examples include a car allowance, private health insurance and free lunch in the company cafeteria. See **fringe benefits**, **net advantages of a job**.

permit
official document that allows an action to be taken, such as a building permit that needs to be obtained before a building can be erected.

perquisite [**per**-kwuh-zit]
See **perks**.

personal accident insurance
an insurance that provides benefits for an individual (or his or her dependants) if they are killed or injured in an accident. See **insurance**.

personal computer
a computer that fits on a desk, and is used by one person at a time. Also known as a PC.

personal identification number
also known as PIN number. A secret number, like a password, that provides access for the use of EFTPOS or a credit card. See **credit card**, **EFTPOS**, **password**.

personal loan
a loan given by a bank to an individual.

personal property
items owned by a person such as money, personal belongings and shares, but not land.

personnel [per-suh-**nel**]
the people employed by an organisation.

petty cash
an amount of money kept in an office to pay small expenses.

petty cash book
a book in which a record of petty cash payments is made.

Phillips curve
an economics concept developed in the late 1950s by an economist called Phillips that states that the lower the unemployment rate in a society the faster the rise in wages and inflation. Similarly, the higher the unemployment the slower the rise in wages and inflation.

phone card
a card that can be purchased and can be used instead of money to make a call using a public phone. The card contains a certain number of units of credit. See **payphone**.

photocopier
a machine that makes photocopies of documents.

piece rate
an amount of money paid for each piece of work. For example, employees are paid per kilogram of coffee beans picked.

pie chart
a circular chart divided into sectors representing the proportion of each value. For example, the circle can be divided into sections representing the proportion of a country's total exports to each of different countries. See **Fig. 57** (above right).

PIN
See **personal identification number**.

Figure 57 Pie chart showing percentage share of Papua New Guinea exports by destination

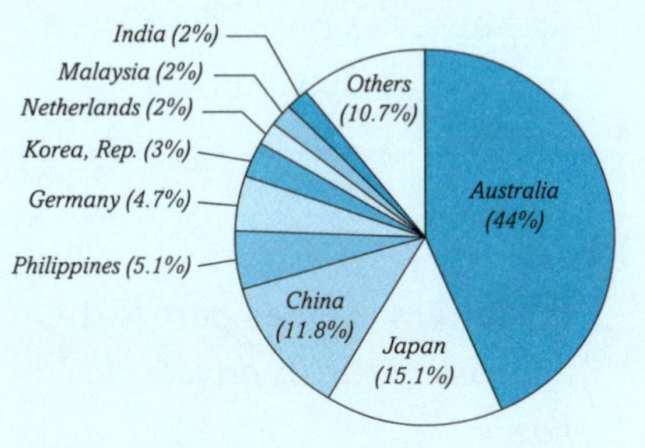

planned economy
See **centrally planned economy**.

planned obsolescence
[ob-suh-**les**-uhns]
the manufacture of consumer products in such a way that they become out-of-date or useless within a known time period so that consumers will have to buy a replacement.

plant
machinery and equipment used in the manufacturing processes.

plough back
to use the profits of the business to expand the business instead of paying

them out to the owners of the business, or paying dividends to shareholders of the companies. See **internal finance**, **reserves**, **retained profits**, **undistributed profits**.

PMB

the letters used as part of the address to mean *private mail bag*.

point elasticity

the ratio of the percentage change in one variable to the percentage change in another. The percentage change in the two variables is calculated relative to their original value. See **elasticity**, **arc elasticity**, **Fig. 37** (p. 102), **Fig. 38** (p. 102).

point elasticity of demand

the ratio of the percentage change in quantity demanded of a good to the percentage change in price, as calculated by the point method. See **elasticity of demand**, **point elasticity**, **Fig. 37** (p. 102), **Fig. 38** (p. 102).

point elasticity of supply

the ratio of the percentage change in quantity supplied of a good to the percentage change in price, as calculated by the point method. See **elasticity of supply**, **point elasticity**, **Fig. 37** (p. 102), **Fig. 38** (p. 102).

policy

a statement of the ongoing and proposed actions of an organisation or government to help reach its long term goals.

poll

1 an activity in which several or many people are asked a question or a series of questions in order to get information about what people think about something.

2 the action of voting in an election and the record of the total number votes that were cast.

poll tax

a tax levied on all citizens which is the same whether the person is receives an income or not. Examples include a council tax or head tax.

polluter pays principle

the principle that the cost of social and environmental pollution should be met by those who cause the pollution. An example is the carbon tax. See **carbon pricing**, **carbon tax**, **greenhouse gas**, **negative externalities**, **pollution**.

pollution

damage to the environment caused by the emissions of dirt, chemical substances and radiation. Air and water pollution resulting from economic activities are the main source of the external costs of production. See **climate change**, **externalities**, **global warming**, **greenhouse gas**, **negative externalities**, **ozone layer**.

population

all of the people inhabiting a specified area. Of the approximately 10 million people living in the South Pacific region in 2013 (ignoring Australia and New Zealand), 7.5 million live in Papua New Guinea. The other 2.5 million live in nine independent nations and a similar number of dependent territories. Nauru and Tuvalu are the smallest of the independent nations of the region with populations of approximately 10 000 and 11 000 people respectively.

population pyramid

graph showing the age structure of the population See **age-sex pyramid**, **Fig. 5** (p. 10).

portfolio

all the different investments held by a person or organisation.

positive externalities

effects of economic activities that result in benefits for people other than the buyers or sellers (third parties). For example, a beekeeper keeps bees to produce honey. The bees pollinate crops in surrounding farms, adding value to the produce of the farmers. Cycling to work helps to reduce the level of pollution and road congestion.

Other road users have quicker journey times and society benefits by the reduced level of pollution. See **externalities**, **negative externalities**.

post office box
numbered boxes at a post office which are rented out to individuals or businesses and where letters for them are kept until collected. Box holders can collect their mail at any time.

postage
see **postal charges**.

postal charges
the charges for posting mail of various types.

postcode
a system of numbers and/or letters attached to a postal address to help with the sorting of mail. Also called a postal code. See **zip code**.

post-date
to put a date on a letter or cheque later than the date on which the document is written. See **post-dated cheque**.

post-dated cheque
a cheque that that is dated for some time in the future. The cheque cannot be cashed or banked until the date on the cheque. See **post date.**

poste restante [pohst ress-**tahnt**]
French phrase meaning 'mail remaining'. A place in a post office where letters or parcels can be sent and kept until they are collected by the person to whom they are addressed.

post-free
pre-addressed envelope with the postage already paid, so that people can send a reply at no cost to themselves.

pp
abbreviation for the Latin term *per procurationem*, which means 'on behalf of' or 'with the authority of'. A letter signed by someone on behalf of an organisation will have pp in front of the name of the organisation and the signature underneath.

practice

the work of a professional person such as an accountant, a lawyer, a doctor, a dentist.

predatory pricing [**pred**-uh-tohr-ee]

pricing goods at a very low price with the intention of driving competition out of the market. While this is good for consumers in the short term it could lead to a monopoly situation in which prices can then be raised and consumers have no choice. See **price war**.

preference share [**pref**-ruhns]

a share in a company that carries no voting power but whose dividends are paid before those on ordinary shares.

preferential creditor [pref-uh-**ren**-shuhl]

a creditor who must be paid before ordinary creditors. Employees are preferential creditors and their wages must be paid before ordinary creditors. See **creditor**.

preliminary expenses

the initial expenses when a company is being formed.

premises [**prem**-iss-ez]

a house or building and the land on which it is built.

premium [**pree**-mee-uhm]

see **insurance premium**.

prepaid

paid in advance.

president

the elected head of a club or society or professional association.

press

newspapers, magazines and the sections of television and radio that broadcast news, and the journalists who work for them.

price

the amount of money paid per unit for a good or service. Price is usually set, though discounts can often be obtained for the purchase of large quantities or by customers haggling with sellers to change the price.

See **bargaining, discount, haggling**.

price competition

beating the competition by offering a lower price.

price controls

government entering the free market to set minimum or maximum prices by law and thus preventing the market from reaching equilibrium. Governments usually use price control for a few essential goods for which they set limits on, or totally ban, price rises.

price–earning ratio (P/E ratio)

the ratio of the current market value of a company's ordinary share to its most recent income (dividend) per share. For example, if the price per share on the stock market is K10.00 and the most recent dividend per share was K1.00, then the price earnings ratio is 10:1. See **dividend**, **share price**.

price elasticity

the ratio of the percentage change of the quantity of a good or service supplied or demanded to the percentage change in price. See **elasticity**, **price elasticity of demand, price elasticity of supply**, **Fig. 38** (p. 102), **Fig. 39** (p. 103).

price elasticity of demand

the ratio of the percentage change of the quantity of a good or service demanded to the percentage change in price. See **arc elasticity of demand**, **elasticity**, **elasticity of demand**, **point elasticity of demand**, **Fig. 38** (p. 102), **Fig. 39** (p. 103).

price elasticity of supply

the ratio of the percentage change of the quantity of a good or service supplied to the percentage change in price. See **arc elasticity of supply**, **elasticity**, **elasticity of supply**, **point elasticity of supply**, **Fig. 38** (p. 102), **Fig. 39** (p. 103).

price index

the ratio of the cost of an individual good (or a basket of goods) to the cost of the same goods purchased at some time in the past, called the base period. The index follows the relative changes in the price of the individual good (or the basket of goods) over time. See **basket**, **consumer price index (CPI)**, **retail price index**, **Fig. 24** (p. 67).

price-maker

a firm that sets the price of goods, services or securities by offering to buy or sell at an announced price. A company that is a price-maker must, as a seller, hold enough stock or be able to produce sufficient quantities to satisfy customer needs. A company that is a price-maker must, as a buyer, have the money to buy all goods being offered by sellers. See **price-takers**.

price support

government policies to maintain prices of a commodity above a minimum price. This occurs mainly for agricultural products where governments either buy products to keep the price from falling or pay producers a subsidy to raise the level of farmers' income. See **floor price**.

price-takers

small-scale sellers who accept the price of the market and are able to sell all their produce without affecting market prices.

price war

a situation in which one or more suppliers charge very low prices to damage the profits of competitors. A price war can occur when demand has reduced and there is surplus production capacity or when one company wants to financially weaken another so that it will accept a takeover offer or to drive it out of business completely. See **predatory pricing**.

primary industry

See **primary sector**.

primary production

See **primary sector**.

primary sector

that part of the economy that makes direct use of natural

resources and includes agriculture, forestry, fishing, mining, and extraction of oil and gas. The primary sector is the first step in the chain of production. Also called primary industry. See **agriculture sector**, **chain of production**, **primary production**, **secondary sector**, **tertiary sector**, **Fig. 18** (p. 50).

principal

1 the amount borrowed or still owing on a loan, separate from interest.
2 the original amount invested, separate from earnings.
3 the owner of a private company.

printout

a page or pages of printed material from a computer's printer.

private company

a company whose shares cannot be offered for sale to the public.

private branch exchange

a telephone exchange within an organisation that connects internal extension numbers to each other or to outside telephone networks. Also called a PBX.

private-enterprise economy

See **capitalism**, **free-market economy**.

private goods

Goods and services that must be purchased in order to be consumed. See **excludable goods**, **public goods**, **rival goods**.

private mail bag

a service offered by the post office to a large organisation in which the post office puts all the organisation's mail into a special mail bag that can be collected by the organisation.

private property

assets held by an individual as part of their personal wealth. The legal protection of private property is the foundation of capitalism and the free-market economy. See **capitalism**, **free-market economy**.

private–public partnerships (PPP)

a public service that is funded and operated through a partnership between government and one or more private sector companies. PPPs are successfully delivering public services such as transport (roads, harbours and airports), prisons, water and electricity in many Pacific countries.

private sector

the part of a country's economy that is not owned by the government.

private wealth

See **private property**.

privatisation

[pry-vuh-tyz-**ay**-shn]

the transfer of state-owned assets into private ownership. Privatisation can raise revenue for governments or spread private ownership of property as happens when government owned houses are publicly sold.

proceeds

the money received from selling something.

produce

1 to make or manufacture goods or services from inputs of production.
2 agricultural and other natural products.

producer

an individual or company that grows or makes things. In economics, a producer is said to combine economic resources (factors of production) in the production process to produce outputs. See **factors of production**.

product

a term used to describe both goods and services.

product liability

part of a public liability insurance policy covering producers in case their products cause harm to a person. For example, a person may become ill from eating a pie, and may demand compensation from the company making the product. See **insurance**.

producer good

a capital good that is used in the production of goods

and services. See **capital good**, **consumer good**, **intermediate good**.

producer surplus

the difference between the minimum price a producer would accept to supply a given quantity of a good and the price actually received.

producers' goods

See **capital goods**.

product differentiation

a marketing process by which producers try to show consumers that their products are different and better than similar goods or services offered by other producers.

production

any activity designed to grow, make or provide goods or services that satisfy consumer needs and wants. In economics, production is the process used to change inputs (factors of production) into outputs (goods and services). See **producer**.

production possibility curve

See **Production Possibility Frontier (PPF)**.

production possibility frontier (PPF)

an economic model that assumes that an economy can only produce two goods and that all of the economy's resources are used to produce these two goods. The PPF, also called the production possibility curve, shows the various combinations of amounts of each of the these two goods that could be produced. Because all the available resources are being used, increasing the production of one good can only happen if production of the other good is reduced. See **model**.

production process

turning resources into finished goods or services.

productivity

output per unit of input. Examples include the crop harvest per unit of land (*tonnes per hectare*), work completed per worker (*output per person per hour*) or total output per day from a factory (*output per day*). Measuring productivity is used as a guide to see whether production is becoming more or less efficient.

profession

a paid occupation, especially one that involves long training, such as an engineer, scientist, economist, lawyer or dentist.

professional association

also called a professional body, professional organisation, or professional society. An organisation whose members belong to the same profession. The organisation is usually formed to control entry into the profession, maintain standards, encourage discussion and professional growth, and represent the profession in discussions with other bodies such as government.

profit

the excess of total sales over total expenses. Profit is the motive for economic activity.

profitable

an activity that makes a profit.

profitability

a measure of how profitable an activity is. The profitability of a company is often measured by its price to earnings ratio. See **price–earning ratio (P/E ratio)**.

profit and loss account

the annual account that shows how much profit or loss has been made. It may be produced more frequently, such as monthly. Sometimes referred to as a revenue statement.

profit centre

the parts of an organisation that are expected to make a profit.

profit margin

the amount of profit made on a particular sale.

profit maximisation

the aim of making as much profit as possible from a business.

pro-forma invoice
an invoice that is sent without the goods being delivered and which does not demand payment. It is used to indicate what the goods or services are going to cost. An actual invoice is sent when the goods are delivered. See **invoice**.

program
a computer program is a list of instructions that enables a computer to carry out a function such as word processing. Without programs, computers are useless.

programmer
a person who writes computer programs.

programming language
a system of coded instructions used to write computer programs.

progressive tax system
a tax system where taxpayers with higher incomes pay higher tax rates than taxpayers with lower incomes. See **proportional tax system**.

progress payment
a payment of part of the full price made to a contractor for work carried out up to a specified stage of the job.

promissory note
[**prom**-uh-sohr-ee]
a document in which a debtor promises to pay an amount of money to a creditor by a certain date.

proportional tax system
[pruh-**pohr**-shuhn-l]
sometimes called a flat tax. A tax system that applies the same rate of tax to all taxpayers, whether they are low, middle or high-income earners. See **progressive tax system**.

property
land, or land and buildings.

proposal form
the form that needs to be completed by a person who wishes to take out an insurance policy.

proprietor [pruh-**pry**-i-ter]
an owner of a business.

proprietorship
a legally established business owned by a single person. The owner or proprietor is entitled to all the profits of the business but is personally responsible for any debts that the company is unable to repay.

prospectus [pruh-**spek**-tuhs]
a booklet that gives information about a share offering (new shares to be issued). It is a formal legal document that provides details such as a description of the company's business, financial statements, biographies of officers and directors, the exact number of shares being issued and their offering price. Such a prospectus will often include an application form for investors wanting to buy shares.

protectionism [pruh-**tek**-shuh-niz-uhm]
the practice of protecting domestic industries from foreign competition by imposing import duties or quotas. See **barriers to trade**, **import quota**, **quota**.

proxy [**prok**-see]
the authority to represent someone else, especially in voting

proxy vote
a vote cast by one person on behalf of another. Proxy votes are usually allowed at a company meeting by which shareholders can nominate another shareholder who is attending the meeting to vote on their behalf.

public company
also called public corporation. A company whose shares are freely traded on a stock exchange.

public corporation
See **public company**.

public goods
goods and services that are provided by the government and used freely by everyone. They include such things as law and order, public parks and street lighting. See **merit goods**, **non-excludable products**, **non-rival goods**,

private goods, **public service**.

public liability insurance

type of insurance that protects a business against compensation claims made by a customer or member of the public should they suffer a loss or injury as a result of its business activities.

public relations

maintaining a good public image of an organisation or individual.

public sector

the part of the economy concerned with providing basic government services. In most countries the public sector includes such services as the police, military, public roads, public transport, education and healthcare. See **merit goods**, **non-excludable products**, **non-rival goods**, **public service**.

public works

construction projects paid for by the government. Includes such public goods as roads, bridges, schools and hospitals.

publisher

an individual or organisation that publishes books and other material.

purchase

to buy.

purchasing officer

the employee of an organisation who is responsible for the buying of goods and services required by the organisation.

purchasing power

the amount of goods and services that a set amount of money can buy. For example, if rice costs K1.00 a kilo then K11.00 will buy 11 kilos of rice. However, inflation causes the price of goods and services to rise. If the cost of a kilo of rice rises to K1.10 a kilo then K11.00 will only buy 10 kilos of rice. As prices of goods and services rise with inflation, the purchasing power of money goes down. See **consumer price index (CPI)**, **inflation**, **real income**, **Fig. 24** (p. 67), **Fig. 60** (p. 219).

put

See **put option**.

put option

offering a contract that will give an investor the right (but not the obligation) to sell a specific share at a fixed price, called the strike price, within a specific time. Investors wanting to sell the contract are required to pay a non-refundable premium for the right. For example, an investor offers a put option contract to sell a share that is currently valued at K10 for the same price in three months' time. He offers a premium of K1 per share upfront to anyone buying his option. The investor is hoping that the share will lose value. If in three months' time the share value has fallen to K5 then the investor can buy these shares in the market for K5 and sell them for K10 to whoever bought his put option. The investor will make a profit of K5 per share, less the premium of K1 he paid. If at the end of three months the price of the shares is more than K10 then the investor can decide not to exercise his option to sell and simply lose his K1 premium. See **call option**, **derivative**, **options contract**.

pyramid scheme

investment scheme in which investors are promised a high rate of returns if they recruit new members. Such schemes are not genuine and can pay the promised returns to a few customers in the early days, but as fewer people join they collapse and most of the people will lose all the money they invested.

quality control

a system for checking the quality of a product before it is sold.

quango [**kwang**-goh]

acronym for *quasi-autonomous non-government organisation*, which is an organisation set up and financed by government and run by a government-appointed board of directors.

quantity demanded

the quantity of a good demanded at any given price. A demand curve plots the change in demand as price changes. See **demand curve**, **Fig. 31a** (p. 85).

quantity supplied

the quantity of a good supplied at any given price. A supply curve plots the change in supply as price changes. See **supply curve**, **Fig. 63a** (p. 245).

questionnaire [kwes-chuh-**nair**]

a printed list of questions sent or given to people, to find out about their attitudes and opinions regarding the services and products provided. See **market research**, **poll**.

quick assets ratio

a measure of a company's short-term liquidity. It compares the value of a company's cash or other assets

Figure 58 Quick assets ratio

$$\text{Quick assets ratio} = \frac{\text{Total value of current cash and other liquid assets}}{\text{Total current liabilities}}$$

that can be changed into cash quickly (liquid assets) with liabilities payable immediately. See **liability**, **liquid assets**, **Fig. 58** (p. 214).

quota [**kwoh**-tuh]
a set amount. An example is a limit placed by government on the quantity of a good that may be imported. See **import quota**, **protectionism**, **sales quota**.

quotation [kwoh-**tey**-shn]
a written or verbal estimate of the cost for a job or a service to be provided.

quote [kwoht]
to give someone an estimated price for a job or a service to be provided.

quoted company
a company whose shares can be bought or sold on a stock exchange. See **public company**, **share**, **stock exchange**.

quoted price
the official price of a share listed on the stock exchange. See **share price**, **stock exchange**.

quoted share
a share that can be bought or sold on a stock exchange. See **share**.

RAM

acronym for *random-access memory* in a computer. It is the part of a computer memory where information is temporarily stored for quick access. The data in RAM stays there only as long as the computer is running. When the computer is turned off, RAM data is lost.

range

in statistics, this is the difference between the lowest and highest values.

rate

a quantity measured with respect to another. Examples include a tax rate of 30 cents in the dollar, a pay rate of K10 per hour or a speed of 40 kilometres per hour.

rate of exchange

See **exchange rate**.

rate of interest

the percentage of the sum of money the borrower pays the lender for the use of the money borrowed. Banks pay interest on deposits and charge interest on loans. See **compound interest**, **interest**, **simple interest**.

rate of return

the annual income from an investment expressed as a percentage of the original investment. See **Fig. 59** (below).

ratio [**ray**-shee-oh]

the result of dividing one number by another. Ratios are used extensively in economics to show

Figure 59 Rate of return

$$\text{Rate of return} = \frac{\text{Annual income}}{\text{Original investment}} \times 100$$

relationships between variables as in measuring elasticity or in describing the relationship between two amounts such as in the ratio of current assets to current liabilities.

rational [**rash**-uh-nl]

1 based on reason or logic, such as a decision based on facts and not on emotions or feelings.
2 having the ability to reason or think about things in a clear, sensible manner.

rationalisation [**rash**-uh-nl-yz-**ey**-zhuhn]

reorganisation to improve efficiency. For example, when production that was previously spread out over many factories is concentrated into fewer locations. The word rationalisation is often used when staff numbers are being reduced.

raw materials

the products of the primary sector that are used as inputs in production. Raw materials include plant products such as cotton, animal products like wool or leather, and ores mined from the earth. See **primary sector**.

re

abbreviation for *with reference to.*

read-only memory (ROM)

the part of a computer memory that contains information that can be read but cannot be altered. It stores programs that will carry out certain functions.

ready cash

banknotes and coins that can be used for immediate payment.

real estate

land and buildings.

real estate agent

a person who sells land and buildings on commission.

real GDP

See **real gross domestic product**.

real GNP

See **real gross national product**.

real GNI

See **real gross national product**.

real gross domestic product (real GDP)

GDP (also called nominal GDP) measures the value of all final goods produced (output) in a country during a given year using the prices during that year. Prices tend to rise due to inflation leading to an increase in GDP from one year to the next, even if the output of goods and services is unchanged. Real GDP measures the value of output in two or more different years by valuing the goods and services adjusted for inflation. For example, if inflation (price increase) was 3% and the output (volume of goods and services produced) was unchanged then while the nominal GDP will have risen by 3%, the 'real GDP' would remain the same. Real GDP gives a more accurate view of the economic growth of a country. See **real income**, **Fig. 60** (p. 219).

real gross national income (real GNI)

a measure of a country's GNI adjusted for inflation. See **gross national income**, **real gross domestic product**, **real income**, **Fig. 60** (p. 219).

real gross national product (real GNP)

a measure of a country's GNP adjusted for inflation. See **gross national income**, **real GDP**, **real income**, **Fig. 60** (p. 219).

real income

the income of an individual or country adjusted for inflation. Take for example a situation in which a worker earns K100 a week. If inflation rose 10% in the year it would mean that general prices of goods will rise by 10% and the worker would now need K110 to purchase the same amount of goods. If however the worker still earns only K100 a week it would mean that while his or her nominal income is still K100 his

Figure 60 Relative value (purchasing power) of a 2005 $US for the period 2005–2013

Year	2005	2006	2007	2008	2009	2010	2011	2012	2013
Value	$1.00	$0.99	$0.94	$0.91	$0.89	$0.90	$0.87	$0.85	$0.83

real income or purchasing power has dropped by 10%. The chart below shows the comparative value (purchasing power) of a 2005 US$1.00 for the period 2005–2013 as calculated using the US CPI. See **purchasing power**, **Fig. 18** (p. 50), **Fig. 60** (above).

realise [**ree**-uh-lyz]

to sell.

realisable value

the amount something can be sold for.

realised loss

the amount lost when a good or service is sold for less than cost price.

realised profit

profit that is in the hand or in the bank. See **paper profit**.

real output

See **real GDP**.

real property

land and buildings.

real value (of money)

See **real income**.

rebate [**ree**-bayt]

1 a part refund of money to someone who has paid too much, such as tax or rent.
2 a discount.

receipt [ri-**seet**]

a document confirming payment and amount received.

receivable [ri-**see**-vuh-buhl]

the amount owed to a business. Receivables are counted as part of the company's assets.

receiver

a person appointed by a bankruptcy court or a creditor such as a bank to manage a company in financial difficulties for the main aim of repaying money owed to creditors.

receivership

the state of a company in the control of a receiver. The receiver will remain in control until such time as he or she has collected cash and paid the creditors who appointed him and then handed back the management of the company to the directors. If this cannot be done, the company will go into liquidation (the business will close down), and pay off whatever debts it can. See **compulsory liquidation**, **liquidation**, **receiver**.

receptionist

a person who answers the phone and attends to customers in an office or a hotel.

recession [ri-**sesh**-uhn]

declining national economic activity lasting more than a few months, during which there is reduced industrial production, employment and real income. A recession is generally defined as a fall in GDP in two successive quarters. See **gross domestic product**.

recycling

the reuse of goods that have served their original purpose, such as empty bottles, empty tins, broken-down cars and used paper, in the production of new goods. Recycling can lower costs and benefit the environment. See **pollution**.

red

see **in the red**.

redeem

to repay a debt.

redeemable preference share

shares issued by a company for a fixed period of time after which the company will buy them back at a previously set price called the redemption value. As with all preference shares, holders cannot vote at shareholder meetings but dividends are paid on these shares before those on ordinary shares.

redemption [ri-**demp**-shn]

the repaying of a debt.

redemption date
the date on which a loan is due to be paid or the date on which a company will buy back redeemable preference shares. See **redeemable preference share**.

red tape
excessive forms, procedures and formalities that seem unnecessary but are required by government or other organisations in order to get things done.

reducing balance
method of calculating depreciation in which the annual depreciation is calculated on the reducing value of the asset. For example, if an asset that costs K1000 is depreciated at 10% per annum, the depreciation in year 1 is 10% of K1000 = K100, reducing its value to K900. In Year 2 the depreciation is calculated on the reduced value of the asset which is 10% of K900 = K90, and so on each following year.

redundancy
[ri-**duhn**-duhn-see]
the dismissal of an employee without any fault on their part. Employees are made redundant when the company no longer carries out the business they were employed for.

redundancy pay
a sum of money given by an employer to an employee who has been made redundant. See **redundancy**.

referee
a person willing to provide a written statement about the character and ability of someone, especially someone applying for a job.

reference
a written testimonial from a referee. See **referee**.

refer to drawer
the words or initials (R/D) written by a bank on a dishonoured cheque See **bounced cheque**, **dishonour**, **dishonoured cheque**.

refinancing
the replacing of a loan with a new loan, usually one with a lower rate of interest.

refund
money given back usually when faulty goods are returned.

register
an official list of names or items such as a list of shareholders of a company.

register of members
a company list of the names of all shareholders and the number and type of stock held by each.

registered mail
mail for which extra postage is paid for safe, secure handling.. Registered mail is recorded at the post office from which it is sent and at the post office to which it is delivered, and is signed for by the receiver.

refusal to deal
an anti-competitive practice by which companies agree not to supply a certain vendor or purchase from a particular seller. See **anti-competitive activities**.

registered office
the official office of a company.

Registrar of Companies
a government official responsible for the keeping of a register of all legal companies and making sure companies lodge all documents and reports required under the Companies Act.

regressive tax [ri-**gres**-iv]
a tax where lower-income earners pay a higher fraction of their income than higher-income earners. A tax on cars is likely to be a regressive tax since lower-income households spend a greater fraction of their income on cars, and thus on the tax on cars.

regulation [reg-yuh-**ley**-shun]
rules and procedures that individuals or companies are required to follow. Example of regulations are those that deal with handling of food for sale, building codes and workplace safety.

reimburse [ree-im-**burs**]
to repay a person who has spent or lost money.

reinsurance
insurance purchased by one insurance company from one or more other insurance companies. By reinsuring, an insurance company spreads the risk of possibly having to make large payouts on insurance claims.

remittance
an amount of money sent from one person to another as a payment or gift. Remittances sent home by family members working overseas are an important financial inflow in many developing countries.

remunerate
[ri-**myoo**-nuh-reyt]
to pay for work.

render
to send an account.

renewable energy
energy resources that are replenished naturally on a human time scale. Solar, hydroelectric, wind, tidal and geothermal power are examples of renewable energy resources. Non-renewable energy resources include fossil fuels such as coal, oil and natural gas. The use of renewable energy reduces the emission of greenhouse gases into the atmosphere. In the past, the use of renewable energy was generally undertaken for environmental rather than economic reasons. However, as fossil fuels become more expensive due to rising prices and anti-pollution measures such as the carbon tax, companies will be more likely to invest in and use renewable energy. See **alternative energy**, **carbon tax**, **carbon trading**, **climate change**, **fossil fuels**, **greenhouse gases**.

renewable resource
a resource that is available on a continuous basis. Examples include agricultural products and renewable

energy. See **renewable energy**.

renewal notice

an advance notice that payment will soon be due to renew something such as an insurance policy, vehicle registration or subscription.

rent

a regular payment made by a tenant to a landlord for the use of land or property.

re-order level

the level of stock at which an order for replacement goods must be made.

report

a written account on some activity.

represent

to act on behalf of someone else.

re-present

present again, such as to bank a cheque that was previously dishonoured.

representative

a person who acts on behalf of another, such as a member of Parliament or a sales representative.

required rate of return (RRR)

minimum acceptable rate of return on an investment proposal that an individual investor or company requires. RRR compares the return with that of a risk-free investment and inflation and therefore helps investors to decide where to invest their money in the proposal. See **net present value**, **Fig. 54** (p. 181).

requisition

[rek-wuh-**zish**-uhn]

a request for something, especially a formal written request on a pre-printed form.

resale price maintenance

where manufacturers have agreements with wholesalers or retailers not to sell a product below a set price. See **anti-competitive practices**.

research and development
the use of company resources to develop new and improved products and more economic methods of production.

reserve price
the price below which something will not be sold at an auction.

reserves
profit of a company not distributed as dividends and held for future expansion of the company. See **retained profits**.

resign
to leave a job.

resignation
the act of resigning.

resolution
a decision by members at a meeting, usually made after voting and approval by the majority of members.

resources
anything that can contribute to economic activity. In economics, resources are defined as a service or other asset used to produce goods and services to meet consumer needs and wants. See **capital goods**, **human resources**, **natural resources**.

retail
sale of goods to consumers.

retail price
the price at which goods are sold to customers.

retail price index
the ratio of the cost of a 'basket' of goods and services bought by an average family to the cost of the same goods and services purchased at some time in the past, called the base period. By following the cost of purchasing the same 'basket' of goods and services over time, the retail price index follows the relative changes in the cost of living for an average family. See **base period**, **basket**, **consumer price index (CPI)**, **price index**, **Fig. 24** (p. 67).

retained earnings
See **retained profit**.

retained profit
the portion of the profits of a company that is retained by the company rather than distributed to shareholders as dividends, See **plough back**, **reserves**.

retire
to stop work because of age or by choice.

return
1 the sending of goods back to a shop.
2 the profit or income from money invested.

returns to scale
a description of the relationship between rate of increase in production (output) and the rate of increase in inputs (factors of production). There are three possibilities:

- Increasing Returns to Scale, where the outputs increase at a rate proportionally higher than the rate inputs are increased. For example, a 25% increase in output for a 20% increase in inputs.
- Constant Returns to Scale, where the outputs increase by the same rate at which inputs are increased.
- Diminishing Returns to Scale, where the outputs increase at a rate proportionally lower than the rates inputs are increased. For example, a 15% increase in output for a 20% increase in inputs.

revaluation
to make a new valuation of an asset. See **book value**, **carrying value**.

revenue [**rev**-uhn-yoo]
1 for a business, income from the sales of goods and services.
2 for a government, money collected by taxation, fees, fines, resource rights and any sales of government property.

revenue expenditure
expenses that are deducted from sales to calculate the profit.

revenue statement
See **profit and loss account**.

reverse charge calls

phone calls which can, by arrangement, be paid by the receiver of the call.

revolving credit

a form of continuous borrowing, whereby as payments are made on a debt, more money can be borrowed. See **credit card**, **overdraft**.

rights issue

an issue of new shares in a company where existing shareholders can, at a special price, buy a number of additional shares proportional to their existing holdings. See **shares**.

rise

1 an increase in number, size, amount, or degree.
2 an increase in an employee's salary or wages.

risk

a situation in which there is a potential for loss, harm or danger balanced against the potential for gain. The probability of the negative outcome can often be calculated or estimated by statistical analysis. See **actuary**, **entrepreneur**.

risk capital

also called venture capital. Funds used for high-risk, high-reward investments such as shares in small mining ventures or new biotechnology companies.

risk management

the practice of identifying and assessing the possible risk for unfortunate situations, and the use of strategies and resources to monitor, control and minimise their probability or the losses resulting, should such events actually take place. See **actuary**, **adverse selection**, **entrepreneur**, **futures**, **hedging**, **insurance**, **reinsurance**, **underwriters**.

rival goods

a private good that when consumed by one person reduces the amount left for others to consume and benefit from. Scarce resources are used up in producing and supplying the good or service. If a mango is eaten then that mango is no longer available to someone else. Similarly, driving a car on a road uses up road space that is no longer available at that time to another motorist. The greater the volume of traffic on the roads, the higher the traffic congestion, reducing average speed and increasing the average journey time for all road user. See **excludable goods**, **private goods**, **public goods**, **non-rival goods**.

robotics [roh-**bot**-iks]
a branch of technology that deals with the design, construction and operation of robots. Robots are machines used in factories to perform high-precision jobs and in situations that would be dangerous for humans such as cleaning toxic wastes or defusing bombs.

rock bottom
the lowest possible price of a good or service or value of a share.

ROM
See **read-only memory**.

round figures
Figures rounded to the nearest 10, 100 or 1000, etc.

royalty
compensation paid to an owner for the use of property, usually copyrighted works, patented inventions, or natural resources. The royalties are usually a percentage of receipts from using the property or a payment for each unit sold.

safe

a strong lockable steel cabinet, for keeping money and valuable documents.

salary

a fixed periodic payment paid by an employer to an employee.

sale

1 the act of selling something.
2 selling items at reduced prices.

sale or return

an arrangement by which a purchaser takes a quantity of goods for resale with the right of returning any goods not sold.

sales

total sales in a business for a period of time, such as a year.

sales analysis

an examination of sales reports to see which goods and services have and have not sold well and to generally measure sales performance by product and area. A sales analysis is also used to make decisions on the stocking of the inventory.

sales conference

a meeting or series of meetings in which all of a company's employees involved in selling its products are told about new products and services and discuss ways in which they can be sold more effectively.

sales drive

an organised effort to increase sales in a business.

sales journal

a record of sales on credit, kept month by month, which is then transferred to the ledger. Debtors are on the debit (left) side and sales are on the credit (right) side of the ledger.

sales manager

the manager who is responsible for the

performance of a team of salespeople.

salesmanship

the ability to understand customer needs and, through a fair and efficient process, persuading them to buy.

salesperson

a person employed to represent a business and to sell its goods and services.

sales promotion

activities that are intended to increase sales. Examples include advertising, giving away free samples and gifts, and sponsoring sports teams.

sales quota

sales targets assigned to individual salespeople, sales teams, dealers, distributors, regions and even countries.

sales representative

a person who sells goods by visiting buyers. The person may receive a commission on the goods sold as well as salary, but sometimes receives commission only.

sales tax

a tax imposed on buyers that is collected by the seller and passed on to the relevant national, provincial, or local-level government.

sales territory

a defined area in which one salesperson, team or distributor will sell the company's product.

salim moni kwik (SMK)

a service offered by Post PNG for fast and safe in-country transfer of money. People can now use their mobile phones to send relatives or friends a PIN number which they then use to collect the money from a post office.

salvage

the rescue of a ship or its cargo from loss at sea.

sample

a small quantity of a product used to show the quality, style, or nature of the whole product. For example, sellers can give customers a small sample of ice cream to tempt them to buy more.

sandwich course

training that is provided to an employee in which courses of study are taken between periods of work.

savings

what is left over of income earned after expenses have been met.

savings and loan society

a society formed by people working for the same firm or in the same industry. Members deposit money and receive interest. The members can also borrow from the society. Examples in Papua New Guinea include the Air Niugini Savings and Loans Society and the Police Savings and Loans Society.

scanner

a device that scans images, text or objects and converts them to digital images that can be stored, edited and displayed on a computer. See **barcode**.

scarcity

in economics scarcity refers to limited resources meaning that there is not enough for everyone to have all they want. People have unlimited wants but do not have the resources to fulfil all their wants. People must therefore make choices between different items. See **choice**, **opportunity cost**.

sea-level rise

a rise in global sea levels caused by factors including the flowing of water into the ocean as glaciers and ice sheets melt. The economic effects of rising sea levels include:

- flooding of low-lying agricultural land;
- reduction of fisheries resources;
- pollution of the freshwater table of low-lying areas and coral islands; and
- destruction of coastal infrastructure and dwellings by flooding and storms.

Rising sea levels threaten the economy and way of life of people in many Pacific nations. See **climate change**, **food security**, **global warming**.

seasonal unemployment
a situation where a number of people are unable to find work during some months of the year. People employed as fruit pickers at harvest time often have difficulty finding jobs when the season is over.

second [**sek**-uhnd]
to support a motion or recommendation at a meeting, thus allowing the motion to be voted on. If passed (supported by a majority), the motion becomes a resolution to be acted on.

second [se-**kond**]
the temporary transfer of a worker from one company or department to another, to carry out a particular task.

secondary sector
manufacturing or processing sector that takes raw materials and converts them into finished goods. Also called secondary industry. See **primary sector**, **secondary production**, **tertiary sector**.

secondary production
the production of manufactured goods from raw materials. See **secondary sector**.

seconder [**sek**-uhnd-uh]
a person who seconds a motion at a meeting.

secondment [se-**kond**-ment]
the act of temporarily transferring a worker from one company or department to another to carry out a particular task.

secret ballot
a written voting method in which a voter's choice is secret. See **show of hands**.

secretarial
[sek-ri-**tair**-ee-uhl]
relating to the work of a secretary.

secretary [**sek**-ri-ter-ee]
1 a person employed to handle correspondence, word processing, filing, and other administrative work for a business office and sometimes as one person's assistant.

2 a person, usually an official, who is in charge of the records, correspondence, minutes of meetings, and related affairs of an organisation, company or association.

sectors

parts of a country's economy involved in similar activities, such as primary producers.

security

a financial instrument that has a known value and can be easily traded. There are generally three types of securities:

- an equity security such as stocks or shares represents part ownership in a cooperation. See **share**, **stock**, **stocks and shares**.
- a debt security such as loans that have been provided to a government or a corporation at a definite interest rate and for a specific period of time. See **bond**, **certificates of deposit**.
- a derivative security such as an option to buy or sell stocks or commodities at a certain price by a specific time. See **derivative option**.

secured creditor

a creditor who, if repayment of a debt has not been made in the required time, can sell some particular asset or assets of the debtor in order to get paid.

self-employed

a person working in business for themself.

self-service

a system such as in a supermarket in which customers select their own goods and take them to a checkout to make payment. See **checkout**.

sell

to make an exchange of goods for money.

seller

a person who sells something.

sellers' market

a market situation in which goods or services are scarce, demand is greater than supply, and sellers can get higher prices.

selling short
See **short selling**.

semi-skilled
a worker with some but not all the necessary skills in a trade or occupation.

service industry
businesses that provide services. See **services**.

services
the provision of intangible (cannot be touched) products such as accounting, banking, consultancy, education and insurance.

settle
to pay a debt or account.

share
a unit of ownership in a company. Owning shares does not give the authority to make day-to-day decisions in the running of the company, however it does entitle the owner to a part of profits, if dividends are paid. See **dividends**.

share capital
the part of a company's capital that has been raised by the sale of shares.

share issues
when new shares in a company are made available to existing shareholders and the public. See **rights issue**.

share certificate
a written document issued on behalf of a company showing legal ownership of a certain number of shares.

shareholder
a person who owns shares in a registered company.

share price
the current price of a single share of a company as quoted by the stock exchange.

share register
a list of shareholders with their shareholding in a company. It is compulsory for all

companies to keep a share register. See **shareholder**.

shelf life

the length of time that goods, especially food items, can be on the shelf in shops and still be fit for sale.

shift

the working period for a group of workers, who work for one part of the day, usually eight hours, and are then replaced by another group.

shipment

a load of goods that are being sent by a company.

shipowners' liability insurance

insurance that protects shipowners against claims for harm caused to people or damage to property. For example, shipowners may become liable for the injury or death of passengers travelling on ships, damage to other ships, or damage caused by oil spillage. See **insurance**.

shipper

a person or company that organises the transport of goods by sea, land or air.

shipping container

See **container**.

shop assistant

a person who serves in a shop.

shoplifting

stealing from a shop.

short (short-position)

1 the selling of a stock, commodity or currency, believing that the value will decline and thus can be bought back later at a lower price. An investor who believes that prices will decrease is called a bear. See **bear**, **long**.

2 the selling of an options contract. See **options contract**.

shortage

a situation in which there is an excess of demand over supply. See **excess demand**.

short delivery
a delivery of a quantity of goods that is less than the quantity stated on the invoice.

shorthand
a fast method of writing by using signs for words. A person expert in shorthand can write at speeds of up to 200 words a minute. Despite being 175 years old, shorthand is still relevant today and used by thousands of journalists, executive personal assistants and secretaries across the world.

short list
the final few applicants being considered for a job.

short run
a period of time in which at least one factor of production has remained fixed. Also called the short term. See **long run**.

short selling
See **short**.

short term
See **short run**.

show of hands
a method of voting in which voters raise their hands showing whether they are voting for or against the motion. See **secret ballot**.

showroom
a room in which goods for sale are displayed.

sick leave
leave granted to employees who are too sick to work.

sight bill
also called a sight draft. A bill of exchange or draft for which money is immediately collected when presented to the person named (the drawee).

signatory [**sig**-nuh-tawr-ee]
a person who is able to sign cheques on behalf of a firm or organisation. There are usually two signatories required for cheques.

simple interest
interest calculated on the principal sum only. See **compound interest**.

site

1 the piece of land on which a building may be built.

2 a website.

skilled

having the training, knowledge, experience and ability to perform a certain activity or task well.

Skype

a computer program that can be used to make free voice and video calls over the Internet to anyone else who is also using Skype. There is a charge for making phone calls to people not on Skype. See **video calling**.

slush fund

a reserve of money that might be used for illegal activities, such as political bribes and other such corrupt dealings.

smartphone

a mobile cellular telephone that also has the ability to connect to the Internet through mobile or WiFi networks. In addition, smartphones provide text messaging, email, Web browsing, still and video cameras, MP3 player and video playback and calling. See **mobile banking**.

smuggle

to bring goods into or take goods out of a country illegally.

soft copy

an electronic copy of data and information stored in a computer. See **hard copy**.

soft loan

a loan made to a country at a low interest rate. Developing countries often receive soft loans from other countries or international agencies as part of development aid packages. See **Asian Development Bank**, **bilateral foreign aid**, **World Bank**.

software

the programs used to run a computer. See **computer software**.

sole agent

a real estate agent who is the only agent that is selling

a property on behalf of the owner.

sole trader

See **proprietorship**.

solicitor [suh-**lis**-i-ter]

lawyer who advises clients and can represents them in the lower courts. See **barrister**, **lawyer**.

solvent

being able to pay all of one's debts.

Secretariat of the Pacific Community (SPC)

formally known as the South Pacific Commission, the SPC is a regional intergovernmental organisation whose main aim is to provide technical, scientific, research and policy services to nations and territories in the Pacific region.

specialisation

concentrating on providing a particular type of goods and services while others provide everything else. Individuals, companies, districts, regions and even whole countries specialise in particular activities.

specification

a detailed description of a product.

speculate

to make investments in stocks, property and other assets with the hope of gaining high returns but with the high risk of loss. See **risk capital**.

spill-over effects

See **externalities**.

sponsor

a person or organisation who supports an individual, organisation, sport or other activity. The support provided can be in cash or by paying for such things as fees, allowances. equipment and training.

spot market

a market in which goods, services, or financial assets are traded for immediate delivery. Different from a futures market, where the delivery will be made at a future date.

spread sheet

a computer program in which data stored in columns and rows can be manipulated and used in calculations.

stabilisation fund

[stey-buh-lyz-**ey**-shn]

a fund set up by a government to keep the price received by producers of agricultural commodities stable or fixed. When prices are high some money is put into the fund and then used to top up what producers receive when prices are low.

staff

the employees of an organisation.

stagflation [stag-**fley**-shn]

a undesirable economic condition in which there is high inflation, slow or stagnant economic growth and a high rate of unemployment. See **deflation**, **hyperinflation**, **inflation**.

stakeholder

a individual or organisation with an interest in something. Owners, creditors, bankers, lenders, employees and unions are all stakeholders in business.

stale cheque

a cheque which will not be honoured by the bank because its date is too old. There may be different time limits applicable in different countries. In Papua New Guinea it is one year.

stamp duty

a tax paid to government on the transfer of ownership documents such as the titles for land and houses and share certificates.

standard of living

often measured in monetary terms such as income per head. However, this does not account for lifestyle. Two people with the same income would be said to have the same standard of living. However, one may live in quiet, peaceful surroundings with clear air, no pollution and little traffic while the other could be living in a crowded, noisy, polluted city with traffic jams and no beautiful scenery. See **gross national happiness (GNH)**.

statement of account

1 a summary of all financial transactions that have occurred in a given period of time in a bank account.

2 a document sent by a supplier to a customer listing all transactions in a given period. It shows all invoices, credit notes, payments and the final balance payable by the customer. See **Fig. 61** (below).

statement of affairs

a list of assets and liabilities of a bankrupt person or a company being liquidated. See **bankrupt**, **liquidate**.

statistics [stuh-**tis**-tiks]

the science of collecting and analysing numerical data.

statutory authority [**stach**-yoo-tawr-ee]

a body set up by the government under an Act of Parliament, to run an activity along business lines. Examples

Figure 61 Statement of account

STATEMENT

31 December 2014

Retailer Ltd
P.O. Box 7777
Boroko

GENERAL SUPPLIERS LTD
P.O. Box 5432
LAE

Date	Particulars	Debit	Credit	Balance
30 Nov 2014	Account Rendered			1000.00
20 Dec 2014	Cash		1000.00	0.00
22 Dec 2014	Invoice 77000	3000.00		3000.00
23 Dec 2014	Invoice 77756	4500.00		7500.00*

* PAYABLE BY END OF JANUARY 2015

include the Papua New Guinea Electricity Commission (ELCOM) and the Solomon Islands Ports Authority.

stock

1 the most common word for inventory, meaning the stock of goods held by a business.

2 generally the same as a share. See **share**.

stockbroker

a person or organisation that buys and sells shares on the stock market on behalf of clients. Stockbrokers charge a fee called a brokerage for every transaction they make on the client's behalf.

stock exchange

a market for the buying and selling of stocks and shares.

stock market

See **stock exchange**.

stocks and shares

See **share**.

stocktaking

the process of counting inventory and listing all stock held.

stock turn

see **stock turnover**.

stock turnover

the rate at which stock is sold. As a general rule, the higher the stock turnover the better the business.

store

a place where goods are kept. Sometimes referred to as a warehouse.

store of value

one of the functions of money allowing people to save current purchasing power to buy goods and services at a future time. See **functions of money**, **money**.

straight-line depreciation

depreciating a fixed or non-current asset by the same amount each year over its estimated economic life.

Figure 62 Straight-line depreciation

$$\text{Annual depreciation} = \frac{\text{Purchase price} - \text{Value at end of economic life}}{\text{Economic life}}$$

Take for example a machine bought for K75 000, expected to have an economic life of five years and then have a residual or scrap value of K10 000.

$$\text{annual depreciation} = \frac{\text{K75 000} - \text{10 000}}{5}$$

$$= \frac{\text{K65 000}}{5} = \text{K13 500}$$

See **Fig. 62** (above).

strike

employees refusing to work, usually because they consider they are not being paid enough, or are not happy with working conditions.

structural adjustment

program of free market and supply-side policies that multilateral agencies such as the IMF require countries to implement as part of the conditions for lending them funds. See **IMF**, **supply-side policies**, **World Bank**.

structural unemployment

unemployment caused by technology changes in an industry such as automation or by a permanent decline in the demand for an industry's product, such as typewriters. See **automation**, **cyclical unemployment**, **frictional unemployment**.

sub-committee

a small committee set up by a council or committee to look into some activity and then report back. For example, a sub-committee to organise a social activity.

subject filing

a filing system in which documents are arranged by subject, such as correspondence and legal matters. See **file**.

sub-lease
the lease of all or a portion of premises by a tenant who has leased the premises from the owner.

subpoena [suh-**pee**-nuh]
a writ ordering a person to attend a court, usually as a witness.

subscription
1 an annual payment to be a member of a club.
2 a periodical payment to receive a magazine, or some other item, on a regular basis.

subsidiary company
a company in which another company, called a holding company or parent company, holds more than 50% of the shares and thus has control of it.

subsidy
money paid by a government to help a producer keep the price of a good or service low. Subsidies also help protect domestic producers against cheaper foreign exports.

subsistence
where a community or individual produces just enough to keep itself or their family at a minimal level. See **subsistence agriculture**, **subsistence economy**.

subsistence agriculture
the type of farming in which most of the product is consumed by the farmer and his family with little or none left over for marketing.

subsistence economy
a situation in which most households consume most of the things they produce with little or none left over for marketing. Societies that use this type of economic system are often rural and farm-based. Also known as a traditional economy, a subsistence economy produces little surplus and is defined by bartering and trading. Subsistence economies were, until recently, very common in Pacific countries but there are very few purely subsistence economies remaining in the region.

subsistence farmer
a farmer who carries out subsistence agriculture.

substitute
any good or service that could be used instead of another. A good is said to be a substitute for another if a rise in the price of one results in a rise in the demand for the other. There is a positive cross elasticity between the two substitute goods. See **cross elasticity**.

substitute goods
See **substitute**.

sue
to take legal action against someone in court.

suitability
See **appropriate capital**.

summons
an order to attend a court to answer a charge.

superannuation
regular payments made by an employee and their employer into a fund aimed at providing future pensions for employees. See **National Provident Fund**.

supermarket
a large self-service store that sells food and a variety of other household goods.

supernormal profit
profits that are greater than those required to keep the producer in business. Supernormal profits usually attract other companies to enter the market.

supervise
to control and manage a group of workers.

supplier
a person or firm that supplies goods or services.

supply
the quantity of goods or services that producers are willing and able to sell at a each of a range of prices at any given time. See **supply curve**, **supply (law of)**, **supply schedule**, **Fig. 63a** (p. 245), **Fig. 64** (p. 246).

supply chain

a network of different companies, often in different countries, involved in the transformation of natural resources and raw materials into intermediate or producer goods and finally into goods for supply to consumers. In a increasingly globalised economy where more production is outsourced to high-skill, low-cost countries, supply chains face many risks. For example, devastating floods in Bangkok in Thailand in 2011 resulted in a global shortage of computer hard drives which lasted throughout 2012. See **outsourcing**.

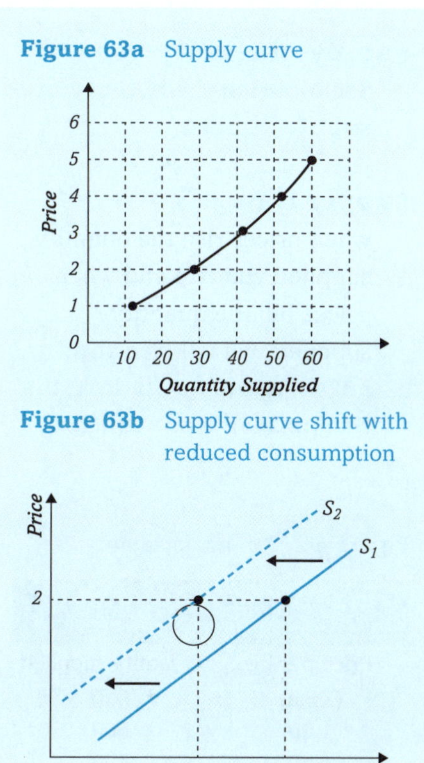

Figure 63a Supply curve

Figure 63b Supply curve shift with reduced consumption

supply curve

a graph of the supply schedule showing the relationship between the quantity of goods or services that producers are willing to supply at each possible price. The supply curve usually slopes upward, since higher prices give producers an incentive to supply more in the hope of making greater revenue.

Other factors affecting supply include the price of other goods, the state of technology, and production costs. The supply curve will shift if any of these factors change. See **determinants of supply**, **elasticity**, **price-elasticity of supply**, **supply (law of)**, **supply schedule**, **Fig. 63a** (above), **Fig. 63b** (above).

supply elasticity

See **elasticity**, **elasticity of supply**, **supply**.

supply (law of)

when prices rise the quantity supplied will rise and when prices fall the quantity supplied will fall. See **supply curve**, **supply schedule**, **Fig. 63a** (p. 245), **Fig. 64** (below).

Figure 64 Supply schedule

Supply schedule for sweet potatoes, one day	
Price per kg (Kina)	Quantity supplied (kg)
1.00	300
1.50	400
2.00	500
2.50	700

supply schedule

a table showing the quantity of a good producers are willing to supply at a range of different prices for a given period of time, all things being equal. See **demand schedule**, **supply curve**, **supply schedule**, **Fig. 63a** (p. 245), **Fig. 64** (above).

supply-side policy

government policies designed to increase supply in the economy. They include improvements in education and training to improve the productivity of the workforce, reducing the power of trade unions, removing regulations that restrict new firms entering the market, and tax reforms that encourage increased production. Supply-side policies are important for long-term economic growth. See **demand-side policy**.

supply lag

time lag between a good or service being demanded and the actual supply of that good or service.

surplus

1 when expenses are less than the income. See **budget surplus**.

2 when output is greater than demand. See **excess supply**.

surrender value

the amount of money that an insurance company will pay

out if a person wishes to cash in an insurance policy before it has run its full term.

suspension
the removal of a person from work for a period of time, usually because the employee has or is suspected of having done something wrong. The employee will be either reinstated or dismissed, depending on the outcome of an investigation.

sustainable development
development that meets the needs of the present without making it difficult for future generations to meet their needs. See **climate change**, **global warming**.

switchboard
telephone equipment for receiving and transferring calls within a business firm.

SWOT analysis
a planning method used to evaluate a proposed project or business venture. The analysis examines the internal strengths and weaknesses of the organisation and the opportunities or threats outside (or external to) the organisation in relation to the project or business venture. The results of a SWOT analysis can direct what steps need to be taken to ensure that the objectives of the project or business venture can be achieved.

syndicate [**sin**-di-keyt]
a group of people or companies who work together for the purpose of making a profit.

systems analysis
studying a process or business to identify its goals and purpose and create systems and procedures that will help achieve them more efficiently.

systems software
See **computer software**.

table
a list of facts and/or figures arranged in columns and rows.

tabulate [**tab**-yuh-layt]
to arrange text or figures in an organised table of columns and rows.

takeover
same as an acquisition, when one company buys another. However, when the word takeover is used it usually means that the company being acquired did not wish to be purchased. See **acquisition**.

takings
the amount of money earned by a business from the sale of goods or services.

tangible asset [**tan**-juh-buhl]
an asset that has a physical form and can be touched. Tangible assets include fixed assets such as buildings, machinery and land and current assets such as stock. See **current assets**, **fixed assets**, **intangible assets**.

tare [tair]
the weight of an empty container or vehicle before goods are packed in or loaded on.

tariff
a tax paid to the government on the import of certain goods and services. It is another word for customs duty.

tax
a compulsory sum of money that must be paid to the government from people's incomes, company profits and the sale of goods. It is the main form of government revenue.

tax burden
the amount of income, property or sales tax paid by an individual or company.

taxable income
the amount of income on which tax has to be paid.

tax assessor
a person employed by the government's tax office, who determines how much tax a person or company is liable to pay. This is done by assessing the tax returns submitted.

taxation
the government system of levying and collecting money from people and businesses.

tax avoidance
the legal avoidance of taxation by organising one's business affairs in such a way as to minimise the amount of tax to be paid.

tax bracket
the rate at which an individual is taxed. Tax brackets are based on income levels. Individuals with lower income levels are taxed at a lower rate than individuals with higher income levels.

tax deductible
an expense that may be deducted from gross income in calculating the amount of tax payable. See **dependents' rebate**.

tax evasion
illegally avoiding the payment of taxation such as by making a false tax return. Penalties and fines may have to be paid on the short-paid tax, and in serious cases may lead to imprisonment.

tax exemption
the freedom from having to pay some or all taxes, as in the cases of charities, international aid agencies, educational institutions and similar organisations. Governments often trying to encourage investment by offering investors tax exemptions. See **tax holiday**, **tax incentive**.

tax form
see **tax return**.

tax free
not subject to tax. An item is made free of tax if it is

included as such in the Tax Act.

tax free allowance
an allowance received by an employee, such as a housing allowance, that is not taxable.

tax haven
a country where few or no taxes are levied. Such a country attracts foreign investors and businesses. Vanuatu is a tax haven.

tax holiday
a limited period of time in which no tax has to be paid. Tax holidays are provided to encourage new investment by individuals or companies.

tax incentive
a reduction in the amount of tax that has to be paid, to encourage investment. See **tax holiday**.

tax inspector
a person who checks on tax returns that seem to give inaccurate information.

tax loss
a loss according to the tax records of a business. The tax loss can be carried into future years and deducted from future taxable profits, reducing tax payable.

taxpayer
a person who pays tax.

tax return
a form completed by a person or business, stating the amount of income earned during the past year, deductions and other tax allowances, and a final calculation of tax to be paid. See **tax assessor**.

tax revenue
the main source of income to government from taxes levied on the incomes of individuals and businesses and on the goods and services produced, exported and imported.

tax threshold
the level of a person's income below which no income tax has to be paid.

tax year

the 12-month period covered by a tax return. This is normally the fiscal year, which in Papua New Guinea is 1 January–31 December, the same as the calendar year. Companies can obtain special permission to have their own tax year such as 1 July–30 June. See **fiscal year**.

technology

the application of scientific knowledge and techniques to improve products and the production process.

telecommunications

worldwide links by telephone, telegraph, cable, satellite, radio and television.

telegraphic transfer (TT)

an electronic method of transferring funds. TTs are usually fairly expensive, due to the bank charges for the transaction.

telemarketing

marketing goods or services to potential customers over the telephone. See **call centre**.

teller

a bank employee who deals with face-to-face transactions with customers.

temp

abbreviation for a *temporary employee*, who does a short assignment in the absence of a permanent employee.

tenant

a person or organisation that rents a building or part of a building.

tender

a formal written offer to supply goods or do a job for an agreed price.

terminal

an electronic device consisting of a keyboard and display screen that is used for entering data into, and displaying data from, a computer or a computing system.

terms

conditions which are offered or accepted, such as the conditions that form part of an employment contract.

terms of trade (TOT)

the value of a country's exports relative to that of its imports. It is calculated by dividing the value of exports by the value of imports, then multiplying the result by 100. If a country's terms of trade (TOT) is less than 100%, there is more capital going out (to buy imports) than there is coming in. If the TOT is greater than 100%, it means that the country is accumulating capital as more money is coming in from exports than going out on imports.

tertiary sector

the part of the economy that produces services such as tourism, banking and insurance. Also called the service industry sector or tertiary industry. See **primary sector**, **secondary sector**.

testimonial

a written account of a person's abilities and strengths by someone who knows the person. Usually written for a prospective employer. See **reference**.

theory of diminishing returns

See **diminishing returns – theory of**.

third party

any individual or group who does not have a direct connection with a situation but who might be affected by it. See **externalities**, **third-party insurance**.

third-party insurance

a compulsory insurance that must be paid for by all motorists that insures the driver of a vehicle against claims for:

- injury to persons in another car or pedestrians.
- damage to other people's property such as another car or fence or building.

See **motor vehicle insurance**.

3G

the third generation of a mobile broadband communication system, which allows smartphones to have fast connection, Internet access, digital photography, graphics transmission and display, and other advanced features. See **4G**, **smartphone**.

tied aid
foreign aid, usually given to developing countries, that is given on the condition that the recipient country uses the funds to purchase goods and services from the donor country.

till
a machine in a shop into which cash from sales is placed. It is called a cash register if it also records the sales.

time card
a card on which times of arrival and departure by employees are recorded using a time clock.

time clock
a machine that records the times of arrival and departure of employees on a time card.

time periods
artificial time periods measured by the extent to which factors of production can or cannot be altered. See **short run**, **long run**.

title deeds
documents that show who is the owner and has legal rights to a property.

toll free call
a business telephone number to which a person may ring free of charge. The business receiving the call pays for the call.

total cost
fixed costs plus variable costs. See **cost curve**, **fixed costs**, **variable costs**, **Fig. 25** (p. 71).

total revenue
the total income of a company from all sources including sales of goods and services.

tourism
a tertiary or service industry that provides information, accommodation,

transportation, and other services to tourists.

track record
a record of a person's or organisation's past performance.

tradeable good or service
good or service that can be sold in another location distant from where it was produced. Such a good or service is said to have tradability. See **non-tradeable goods and services**.

trade
the buying and selling of goods and services.

trade association
an organisation of producers or sellers of similar products or services whose main focus is collaboration and sharing of ideas between members. Such associations also participate in public relations activities such as advertising, education, and negotiating with governments, trade unions and others.

trade barriers
See **barriers to trade**.

trade credit
credit given by suppliers to their customers. It is common to not require customers to pay immediately for goods that have been delivered. The time period allowed could be as short as 30 days for consumer goods and as long as a year for large capital purchases.

trade creditor
a person or business that has supplied raw materials or component parts to a manufacturer and is owed money for them.

trade cycle
See **business cycle**.

trade deficit
a situation where the value of a country's exports is less than the value of its imports. Also called a trade gap.

trade directory
a book that contains information about companies and their products.

trade discount

a discount given by a manufacturer or wholesaler to a retailer.

trade fair

an exhibition where companies display their goods and services, to promote export sales. Trade fairs are usually given government assistance and are often held in foreign countries. See **trade promotion**.

trade gap

See **trade deficit**.

trademark

a name or symbol that is used on the products to enable the public to identify the supplier. Trademarks have to be registered and can be sold. In Papua New Guinea, trademarks are registered with the Trade Marks Division of the Investment Promotion Authority.

trade-off

the process of deciding whether to obtain less of one benefit or good in order to get more of another. A compromise by choice.

trade price

a reduced price paid by a retailer when buying goods from a wholesaler or manufacturer. See **trade discount**.

trade promotion

a marketing exercise to increase sale in a foreign country or to get retailers to stock and support the sale of products. See **trade fair**.

trade surplus

a situation where the value of a country's exports is more than the value of its imports. See **trade deficit**.

trade unions

an organisation of employees formed for the purpose of bargaining with employers on behalf of all employees for better wages and working conditions. See **industrial action**, **industrial dispute**, **industrial relations**, **strike**.

trading bloc

a regional group of countries cooperating together to liberalise trade between each other. See **Pacific Island Countries Trade Agreement (PICTA)**.

traditional economy

See **subsistence economy**.

traditional society

a society based on traditions, customs, and beliefs. Production and consumption are usually based on the needs of subsistence and rituals. People do not work for wages and the division of labor is governed by age, gender, and status. The units of production in a traditional society are the family, the clan and the village. See **subsistence economy**.

train

to teach a person the skills necessary to do a particular job.

trainee

the person being trained.

trainer

the person doing the training.

training manual

a book of instructions designed to assist in the training of employees to improve their performance in undertaking certain tasks.

transact

to carry out a business deal.

transaction

the act of carrying out a business deal.

transaction cost

expenses incurred when buying or selling an asset, over and above the actual cost of the asset. Examples include brokers' or agents' commissions, government taxes and fees such as stamp duties and capital gains tax, and legal and title search fees.

transcript

a written version of information that was originally presented verbally.

transfer earnings

how much a factor of production could earn in its next best use. Take for example a block of land that could earn K2 million a year as a block of apartments. If the owners could not build a block of apartments, the next best use might be building a car park that will earn K600 000 a year. The transfer earnings of the block of land is then K600 000. See **economic rent**.

transfer pricing

the prices of goods and services provided by one part of an organisation to another. This particularly applies to transactions between companies and their subsidiaries in another countries. Transfer pricing allows multinationals to transfer profits from one country to another declaring high incomes and profits in countries with low taxation rates. Transfer pricing often results in the country of originof products such as timber and other raw materials losing possible tax revenue.

transfer payments

payment made by government for which it receives no goods or services. Transfer payments include social benefits such as unemployment benefits, age pensions and subsidies and grants paid to producers. Transfer payments are transfers of income of taxation from one section of society (taxpayers) to another.

transformation

changing of raw materials during the production process into outputs that are required by the market. This requires two sets of resources:

- the transforming resources such as buildings, machinery, computers, and people that carry out the transformation.
- the transformed resources, which are the raw materials and components that are transformed into end products.

transport
moving of people or goods from one place to another.

travel agent
a person or organisation that arranges travel and accommodation for people going on a business trip or on holiday.

travel allowance
money given to employees to pay for expenses on a business trip.

travel expenses
money spent by an employee on a business trip.

treasurer
a person who is responsible for the finances of an organisation.

trickle down
a belief by some economists that economic growth and reductions in taxes that provide financial benefits to large businesses and wealthy investors eventually benefits the poorest in society by increasing the demand for labour.

true and fair view
annual accounts of companies are required, by the Companies Act, to provide a reliable estimate of profits, and a balance sheet which is factual in accordance with International Accounting Standards.

TT
See **telegraphic transfer**.

turnover
another word for sales.

tying
where a seller agrees to sell a buyer a product or service on the condition that the buyer also buys another product. Examples include having to pay for a hotel room that includes breakfast or a washing machine that includes a 12-month service contract. See **anti-competitive practices**.

unanimous
[yoo-**nan**-uh-muhs]
a decision or vote with which everyone is in total agreement.

unappropriated profit
[uhn-uh-**proh**-pree-ey-tid]
See **undistributed profit**.

unaudited [un-**aw**-dit-ed]
accounts that have not been audited. See **audit**.

unbanked
also called underbanked. The more than half of the world's adult population, usually living in rural communities, that have no access to banking facilities. Mobile banking combined with microfinance provides the possibility of making these services available to rural communities. See **microfinance**, **mobile application**, **mobile banking**, **mobile money**.

uncompetitive
unable to sell at a profit. Goods and services may be uncompetitive because their prices are higher than those offered by competitors or because they are of poor quality or defective. High costs may be due to labour or materials being expensive or technology being outdated.

unconditional
without any conditions. For example, an offer made without any conditions.

underdeveloped country
term not in common use. See **developing economy (country)**.

undersigned
referring to the person or persons who have signed a letter.

underwrite
the acceptance by a financial institution of the financial risks involved in a transaction. For example:

- merchant banks underwrite new share issues by

- guaranteeing to buy all shares that are not sold on the open market.
- insurance companies underwrite insurance policies guaranteeing to pay all genuine claims against the insurance policy.

underwriter

a person or firm who underwrites an insurance policy or a share issue. See **underwrite**.

undischarged bankrupt

someone who has been declared bankrupt and who has not been discharged from bankruptcy. A person who is an undischarged bankrupt is banned from holding certain positions such as director in a company. See **bankrupt**.

undistributed profit

profit not paid out in dividends to the shareholders of a company The profit remains in the reserves of the company. See **internal finance**, **plough back**, **reserves**, **retained profits**.

unearned income

a term used by a finance company that has charged interest on hire purchase agreements and lease agreements that still have a period of time to run. Some of the interest will be earned in the future, therefore it is unearned interest.

unemployment

not being able to find a job when one is willing and able to work at current wage rates.

unemployment rate

the number of unemployed as a percentage of the number of people who are employed or unemployed. See **Fig. 65** (below).

Figure 65 Unemployment rate

$$\text{Unemployment rate} = \frac{\text{Number unemployed}}{\text{Number employed} + \text{Number unemployed}} \times 100$$

unitary elasticity
[**yoo**-ni-ter-ee]

also called unit elasticity. A situation in which a change in one variable causes the same percentage change in another variable. Elasticity will have a value equal to 1 (ignoring the negative sign). See **unitary elasticity of demand**.

unitary elasticity of demand

a situation in which a change in price causes the same percentage change in the quantity demanded. Elasticity will have a value equal to 1 (ignoring the negative sign). See **demand elasticity**, **elastic demand**, **elasticity**, **inelastic demand**, **unitary elasticity**, **Fig. 66** (below left).

unitary elasticity of supply

a situation in which a change in price causes the same percentage change in the quantity supplied. Elasticity will have a value equal to 1 (ignoring the negative sign). See **demand elasticity**, **elastic demand**, **elasticity**, **inelastic demand**, **unitary elasticity**, **Fig. 67** (below right).

unit cost

the cost of one unit of output calculated by dividing the total production cost by the number of units produced.

Figure 66 Unitary elasticity demand

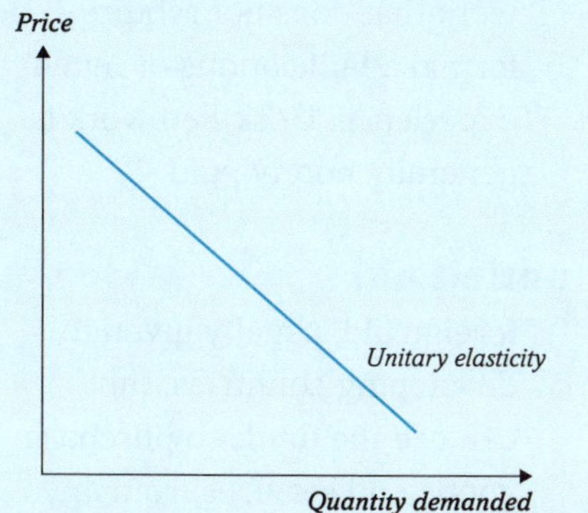

Figure 67 Unitary elasticity supply

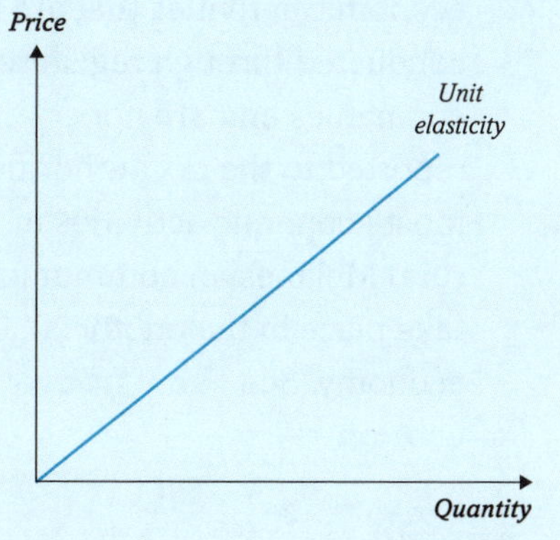

unit elasticity
See **unitary elasticity**.

unit elasticity of demand
See **unitary elasticity of demand**.

unit elasticity of supply
See **unitary elasticity of supply**.

unit price
the price of one unit.

union
See **trade union**.

unlawful
not allowed by law, illegal.

unlisted company
a company which is not listed on the stock exchange.

unofficial economy
economic activities that are not conducted through registered companies and are not reported to the tax authorities. Most economic activities in rural Melanesian communities take place in the unofficial economy. See **subsistence economy**.

unpaid
not yet paid for.

unprofitable
an activity which does not make a profit and may make a loss.

unsecured creditor
an individual or institution that lends money without collateral. See **collateral**, **secured creditor**, **unsecured debt**, **unsecured loan**.

unsecured debt
a debt that is owed and not backed by assets or collateral. See **collateral**, **unsecured creditor**.

unsecured loan
a loan where the creditor has no claim on any assets or other collateral should the debtor default on the loan.

unskilled work
work that does not require formal qualifications or much experience. Unskilled work is generally poorly paid.

untied aid
foreign aid, usually given to developing countries, that can use the funds to purchase goods and services from any country.

upfront
a payment (part or full) that must be made before goods are delivered or services are rendered.

upmarket
something that is expensive and designed for high-income consumers.

upstream integration
See **vertical integration**.

urbanisation
the growth of towns and cities and the migration of rural populations into them. Urbanisation in Melanesia has resulted in unemployment, law and order problems, a shortage of housing and the development of squatter settlements which lack water, sanitation and sewage.

Uruguay Round [**yoor**-uh-gwy]
a round of trade negotiations conducted within the framework of the General Agreement on Tariffs and Trade (GATT) from 1986 to 1994 with 123 countries participating. The Uruguay Round led to the creation of the World Trade Organization. See **Doha Round**, **General Agreement on Tariffs and Trade (GATT)**, **World Trade Organization**.

usufruct [**yoo**-zoo-fruhkt]
system of land tenure common in most of Melanesia, where land is communally owned and people from the community have access to use it.

usury [**yoo**-zhuh-ree]
the practice of charging extremely high interest on loans. Studies of informal money lending in Port Moresby in 2012 reported interest rates of between 10% and 30% a fortnight, which is equivalent to between 250% and 750% a year.

utmost good faith
a condition of an insurance policy in which the person taking out the policy (the insured) must provide all necessary facts to the insurer (insurance company). In turn, the insurer must make sure the policy meets the needs of the insured. This is the opposite of the legal principle *caveat emptor* (let the buyer beware). See ***caveat emptor***.

vacancy
an unoccupied job, position, office or accommodation.

vacation
a holiday or period of leave.

valid [**val**-id]
legally acceptable, such as a valid title, valid contract or valid passport.

valuable
worth a lot of money.

valuation
an estimate of the value or worth of something.

value
the worth of something in money terms.

value added
1 estimated value that is added to a product or material at each stage of its manufacture or distribution:
2 what a firm does when it takes a product that is very similar to that offered by a competitor and provides potential customers with a feature or add-on, such as 12 months' free service, that gives it a sense of greater value.

value added tax
a tax paid by the consumer that is added to the price of goods and some services Also known as VAT.

value for money
used to describe a good or service that is considered worth the price paid.

valuer
a person who carries out valuations.

variable cost
a cost that varies in proportion to the goods or services produced. They rise as production increases and fall as production decreases. Variable cost can include the cost of materials and labour. See **fixed costs**.

variable factors
inputs that can be varied in amount in the short run to either increase or decrease the output of production.

vertical integration
when a producer expands their business into a step before or after in the chain of production. For example, an oil refinery combining with a chain of petrol stations to have outlets for their products. This is also called forward or downstream integration. If a baker combines with wheat producers to make sure they have supplies for their products, it is called backward or upstream integration. See **Fig. 18** (p. 50).

VAT
see **value added tax**.

VDU
see **visual display unit**.

vendor
a seller.

venture capital [**ven**-cher]
See **risk capital**.

video calling
also known as videophone, or video conferencing. Allows people with smartphones or computers and Internet access to talk to and view live video of each other at the same time. Video calling is sometimes used for job interviews. See **interview**, **Skype**.

virus
a program or piece of code that loads itself onto a computer, often through the Internet, and duplicates itself, using up memory, destroying data and eventually even bringing the system to a halt.

visa
an entry in a passport that allows the holder to enter a particular country for a period of time. A visa may be for the purpose of employment, business or tourism.

visible exports
the export of actual goods to other countries. See **invisible exports**.

visible imports

the import of actual goods into a country. See **invisible imports**.

visible trade

the export and import of actual goods to and from other countries. See **invisible trade**, **visible exports**, **visible imports**.

visual display unit

an electronic device, like a television set, used to display the output from a computer. Also called a VDU.

void

not valid or legally binding. See **null and void**.

voluntary liquidation

the shareholders of a company decide to wind up a company which is solvent (able to pay its debts). See **compulsory liquidation**, **liquidation**.

voluntary redundancy

a financial incentive offered by a company to encourage employees to voluntarily resign.

voluntary unemployment

where workers choose not to work because they are not willing to accept the available jobs or the wages being offered. See **involuntary unemployment**.

voting rights

the right of a stockholder to vote on company matters such as who will make up the board of directors. See **proxy**.

voucher

1. in accounting, a document that shows how money has been paid out, and the account in the ledger in which it has been entered.
2. a printed piece of paper that entitles the holder to a discount or that could be exchanged for goods or cash.

wage differentials
different rates of pay for the same general type of work. The differences in pay could be for a variety of reasons including differences in working conditions, performance standards and types of workers being employed.

wage equilibrium
the wage rate at which the demand for labour equals the supply of labour. A rise in demand will result in a rise in the equilibrium wage.

wage earner
a person who works for wages.

wage freeze
a action by government or a company to stop all wage increases for a period of time.

wage negotiations
discussions between employers and employees, or employees' representatives such as unions, about wage levels and wage increases. See **bargaining**, **collective bargaining**, **counter offer**, **negotiate**.

wage packet
See **pay packet**.

wage policy
government policy on setting wages and wage increases for workers, such as the setting of minimum wages.

wage-price spiral
1 when inflation causes demands for higher wages which then results in price rises and further inflation. See **inflation**.
2 wages and prices chasing each other as the aggregate demand curve continually shifts to the right and the aggregate supply curve continually shifts upwards. See **Fig. 19** (p. 51), **Fig. 31b** (p. 85).

wages

1 fixed regular payments paid to workers for services. Wages can be paid daily, weekly, fortnightly or monthly.
2 in economics, the return to the factor of production, labour.

wage scale

the rates of pay for different jobs within a company or public service.

wages clerk

a person in an office who calculates wages and pays them out.

wants

goods or services that a consumer desires but that are not absolutely necessary for survival. Ice cream and music are examples of wants. See **needs**.

warehouse

a place where raw materials or manufactured goods are stored before they are sold.

warranty [**wawr**-uhn-tee]

a written guarantee, provided to the purchaser of a good by its manufacturer, promising to repair or replace the good if it is defective within a certain period of time.

wealth

a measure of the value of all of the assets of worth owned by a person, community, company or country. People are said to be wealthy when they own many valuable resources or goods. The wealth of a country is measured by its gross domestic product (GDP) or GDP per capita. See **gross domestic product**, **per capita gross domestic product**, **Fig. 47** (p. 133).

wealthy

having a great deal of money, resources, or assets.

webpage

a document on the World Wide Web. Every webpage is identified by a unique address called a URL (Uniform Resource Locator). Web documents can contain graphics, sounds, text and video. See **browser**, **Internet**, **website**, **World Wide Web**.

website

place on the Internet that contains information about a person, company, educational institution, government, or organisation. A website normally consists of a group of webpages linked to each other. Many companies have websites that advertise the products and services they supply. See **online shopping**, **webpage**.

weighted average cost

a method for calculating the unit cost of items in stock when different quantities have been purchased at different unit costs. Each time goods are added to the stock, a new average cost is calculated by dividing the total cost of all goods held in stock by the number of units in stock. See **Fig. 68** (below).

welfare state

a system whereby the state undertakes to protect the health and well-being of its citizens, especially those in financial or social need. The state provides health care and education as well as old-age and disability pensions, unemployment benefits and various other means of family support.

wharf

a level area alongside which a ship or boat can be moored to load or unload cargo or passengers.

wharfage

1 the use of a wharf for loading, unloading and storage of goods.
2 charges for the use of a wharf.

Figure 68 Weighted average cost calculation

Stock on hand 100 units @ K5.00 =	K500
Purchases 50 @ K5.10 each	K255
	K755

Therefore, stock is now valued at K5.03 each (K755 divided by 150 units).

whole-of-life policy

a form of insurance in which the insured person pays a fixed amount in premium each year and on their death an insurance payout is made to their beneficiaries.

wholesale

the sale of goods in large quantities, usually to retailers who then sell them to consumers.

wholesale price

the prices at which wholesalers sell to retailers.

wholesaler

a company that buys in bulk from manufacturers, and sells to retailers.

wholly owned subsidiary

a company whose shares are 100% owned by another company called the parent company.

Wi-Fi

a wireless networking technology that uses radio waves to provide wireless high-speed Internet and network connections for computers, smartphones, or other devices. See **wireless router**.

will

a legal document in which a person states how their money, assets and property will be managed or distributed after their death.

winding up

See **liquidation**.

wireless router

connected through a modem to a telephone network, wireless routers have a small transmitter that converts the Internet data coming in through the modem into radio signals. The signals are picked up by computers and smartphones, allowing them to connect wirelessly to the Internet. See **modem**, **Wi-Fi**.

withdrawal

taking money out of a bank account.

withholding tax

in some countries the tax payable on dividends is deducted by the company and paid directly to the government on behalf of the shareholder. In these countries, banks do the same with the tax payable on interest earned by depositors.

without prejudice

words on a letter or document stating that the information it contains is not legally binding and cannot be used in a court of law.

word processing

using a computer to create, edit and print documents. See **word processor**.

word processor

a computer program that enables a computers to create, edit, and format text entered from a keyboard and provide a printout.

words and figures do not agree

written on a cheque being dishonoured because there is a difference in amounts between the words and figures on the cheque.

work

1 employment of people in jobs to make goods or services.
2 what a person does to earn money.
3 the place where a worker carries out their duties.

workaholic

a person who works excessively long hours and tends not to have enough rest or recreation.

work ethics

accepted rules of behaviour by workers.

work force

all the employees in an organisation.

work in progress

goods in the course of manufacture.

work load

the amount of work that a person is required to do.

work permit
an official document that allows a foreigner to work in a country.

work place
the place where people do their work.

work shop
a room or building where goods are repaired or manufactured.

worker
a person who works for an organisation.

working capital
the excess of current assets over current liabilities. It gives an indication of a company's efficiency, its short-term financial health, and whether it will be able to pay its current debts.

See **current assets**, **current liabilities**, **Fig. 69** (below).

working conditions
the conditions in which individuals and staff work. Includes such things as amenities, physical environment, stress, safety, wages and legal rights.

working day
the part of the day in which work is done, normally for around 8 hours, from approximately 8 am till 5 pm.

working hours
hours in which work should be done. Personal affairs should not be attended to during working hours.

World Bank
an institution of the United Nations which provides expertise and lends money to countries to help them with projects and programs aimed at long-term economic development and poverty reduction. See **International Monetary Fund (IMF)**.

Figure 69 Working capital

Working capital = Current assets – Current liabilities

World Trade Organization (WTO)

an international organisation that administers and monitors international trading systems, promotes free trade and seeks to resolve trade disputes between countries. See **Doha Round**, **General Agreement on Tariffs and Trade (GATT)**, **Uruguay Round**.

World Wide Web (Web)

more commonly called the Web. A way of accessing information using the Internet. Users of the Web use browsers such as Internet Explorer or Firefox on their computers or smartphones to access Web documents called webpages. See **browser**, **Internet**, **webpage**.

worthless

having no value.

write-off

1 remove a bad debt that cannot be collected from a company's accounts.
2 reduce the value of an asset in a company's accounts. Depreciation is the method of writing off the value of assets over time. The value of assets destroyed in an accident are written off to zero.
3 amortise goodwill. See **amortise**, **goodwill**.

WTO

See **World Trade Organization**.

year end
the end of the financial year when the annual accounts of a company for the year must be prepared.

yield [yeeld]
1 an agricultural yield is the amount of a crop that was harvested per unit of land area for a given time. Units are usually kilograms per hectareor metric tons per hectare.
2 a financial yield is the income generated by an asset on an annual basis, expressed as a percentage of the asset's purchase or market price. See **price–earning ratio (P/E ratio)**.

Yours faithfully
written at the end of a letter before the signature, for a letter that begins Dear Sir or Dear Madam, when the name of the person to whom the letter is being sent is unknown.

Yours sincerely
used above the signature on a letter addressed with the name of the person.

zero
the figure nought (0) designating no quantity.

zero inflation
no inflation. See **inflation**.

zero rated
in value added tax, an item on which value added tax (VAT) is rated as zero. See **value added tax**.

zip code
post code system used in the United States of America. See **post code**.